DAUGHTERS

OF
SELF-CREATION

DAUGHTERS

OF

SELF-CREATION

THE CONTEMPORARY
CHICANA
NOVEL

ANNIE O. EYSTUROY

University of New Mexico Press / Albuquerque

Library of Congress Cataloging-in-Publication Data
Eysturoy, Annie O., 1955–
Daughters of self-creation : the contemporary Chicana novel /
Annie O. Eysturoy. — 1st ed.
p.   cm.
Includes bibliographical references and index.
ISBN 0-8263-1675-1
1. American fiction—Mexican American authors—
History and criticism.
2. Women and literature—United States—History—20th century.
3. American fiction—Women authors—History and criticism.
4. American fiction—20th century—History and criticism.
5. Self-actualization (Psychology) in literature.
6. Mexican American women in literature.
7. Mexican Americans in literature.
8. Bildungsroman.
I. Title.
PS153.M4E97 1996
813'.540986872073—dc20 95-4419
CIP

To my family

CONTENTS

ACKNOWLEDGMENTS

This study, based upon my American Studies doctoral dissertation, is dedicated to a new voice that has emerged on the American literary scene, the voice of the Chicana. During the course of my doctoral program at the University of New Mexico, I became increasingly interested in the distinctive perspectives that Chicana writers bring to literature, perspectives that have grown out of their historical, bicultural heritage as members of a minority population in a dominant Anglo culture. That interest became the basis for this study, which examines how Chicana writers expand traditional literary paradigms through their exploration of questions of gender, ethnicity, and class.

Many individuals contributed to this study in many different ways. I thank them all. I am particularly grateful to Erlinda Gonzales-Berry, Antonio Márquez, Francisco Lomelí, and Vera Norwood. They all provided helpful readings during the course of this work. Special thanks to Jane Caputi, friend and adviser, for her encouragement and support over the years. I also express my deep appreciation to Teresa Márquez, friend and library guide, for her never-failing helpfulness and hospitality.

Finally, I thank my editor, Andrea Otañez, for excellent editorial advice, and Marta Field for her long-distance word processing assistance.

DAUGHTERS
OF
SELF-CREATION

INTRODUCTION

Women's stories have not been told. And without stories there is no articulation of experience. Without stories a woman is lost. . . . She is closed in silence.
—Carol Christ

Women will starve in silence until new stories are created which confer on them the power of naming themselves.
—Sandra Gilbert and Susan Gubar

A central theme of contemporary Chicana fiction is the quest for authentic female self-development. This process is both environmental and psychological, and it entails coming to terms with multiple social and cultural forces, external as well as internal, that infringe upon the path toward female individuation and an understanding of the individual self. Rites of passage are depicted either as the adolescent protagonist's coming of age, her striving to gain maturity and a vision of her own future, or as the mature woman's awakening to the reality of her social and cultural role as a woman and her subsequent attempts to reexamine her life and shape it in accordance with her new feminist consciousness.

This process of becoming, whether it is that of the child and adolescent or the somewhat older woman, is a recurrent theme in Chicana literature, and due to this very subject matter, many Chicana narratives belong to the *Bildungsroman* genre, the literary form traditionally used to portray the process of self-development.[1] It is significant that it is not solely a search for identity per se that engages Chicana writers, but rather an exploration and articulation of the

3

process leading to a purposeful awakening of the female protagonist. In the case of the child and adolescent protagonist, the emphasis is on social and environmental influences on her rite of passage, whereas narratives with a more mature protagonist tend to be more confessional in nature, emphasizing the reexamination of the past through the recollection of past experiences in order to arrive at an understanding of her female self. In both cases the emphasis is on the education of the self emerging from the interaction between the self and the world.

The *Bildungsroman* usually ends on a positive note in that it constitutes a new beginning for the protagonist, who, having reached a certain stage of selfhood, is ready to profit from her *Bildungs* process and shape her own life in accordance with her awareness and desire for authentic self-fulfillment. This, however, should not overshadow the fact that the *Bildungsroman* is written for the sake of the journey, the exploration of the path toward self-development, and not for the sake of any positive denouement that could be the outcome of this process.

The path toward self-development or self-definition is in some cases portrayed as intimately connected to the process of creation; thus the act of writing or creating becomes essential to discovery of self. These particular aspects, the intersections of self-development and creativity, qualify some Chicana *Bildungsromane* as *Künstlerromane*. The latter is a form of the *Bildungsroman* that portrays the development of an individual who becomes—or is on the threshold of becoming—an artist of some kind. Traditionally the hero of the *Bildungsroman* may dream of becoming an artist, but ultimately settles for a conventional life, whereas the *Künstlerroman* hero usually rejects such commonplace prospects and opts for a life devoted to artistic endeavors. These two literary classifications often intermingle in that the *Bildungsroman* is generally perceived to contain some degree of autobiography; the artistic inclinations of the protagonist in some of these development novels is thus only a natural reflection of the sensitivity of their authors and of the autobiographical tendency of the genre. However, this study will not take into consideration biographical details external to the works themselves but will analyze how Chicana authors portray the process of self-development, and in the cases to which it applies, will also analyze how the concept of discovery of self is connected with the process of creation.

Chicana *Bildungsromane* partake in a general trend in contemporary women's literature: during the last three decades women writers have often adapted the basic patterns of the traditionally male-defined *Bildungsroman,* but given the particular nature of female development, women's *Bildungsromane* have transformed the concept of *Bildung* and thereby also the traditional definitions of the genre. Before turning to Chicana novels of self-development, it is therefore appropriate to examine the basic concepts of the *Bildungsroman* tradition and the belated emergence of the female *Bildungsroman* in order to establish the historical and critical literary context for the Chicana entry into this literary tradition.

As a category of the novel, the *Bildungsroman* is a narrative form characterized and defined by its subject matter. It is the particular perspective of the protagonist, his or her inner development, and not an identifiable structure, that defines a *Bildungsroman;* in other words, it is defined "by its inner rather than by its outer form" (Jost, 150). The unifying concept of the *Bildungsroman,* its defining characteristic, is the singular attention this genre pays to the growth and development of the protagonist. This development emerges from an interaction between the protagonist and the world; it is the protagonist's response to his or her particular environment, the interplay between social and psychological forces, that determines the direction of each individual process of self-development. This interplay between the self and the world is usually revealed through events that have had a particular influence on the formation of the protagonist, moments or specific experiences rather than a full account of the protagonist's life.

The *Bildungsroman* is also perceived to be a didactic novel. This particular aspect of the genre was already indicated by Karl Morgenstern, who in his definition of this narrative genre coined the literary term *Bildungsroman* in the early 1820s:

> It will justly bear the name *Bildungsroman* firstly and primarily on account of its thematic material, because it portrays the *Bildung* of the hero in its beginnings and growth to a certain stage of completeness; and also secondly because it is by virtue of this portrayal that it furthers the reader's *Bildung* to a much greater extent than any other kind of novel. (from Köhn, 431)

The *Bildungsroman* is a product of the imagination and portrays an individual growth process that posits an alternative model to prevailing perceptions of being. The imagination of the protagonist plays a crucial role in this process, as this faculty enables him or her to transcend the limitations of social reality. This imaginative search for an existence that goes beyond what is given constitutes the true *Bildung* of the protagonist, and possibly also the education of the reader, and reflects again the particular artistic sensitivities of the individual authors. The generally hopeful ending of the *Bildungsroman* underscores the feasibility of an alternative path toward self-development.

Society becomes the locus for experience and to some extent the antagonist of the *Bildungsroman*. The protagonist has to measure his or her emerging self against the values and spirit of a particular social context, representative of an age and a culture. The environmental character and its influence on the protagonist reveals aspects of the zeitgeist of the individual work; the particular *Bildung* of the protagonist, its possibilities, prospects, or limitations, reflects to a

Introduction

great extent the spirit of the time and place in question. The Aristotelian dictum that the human being is a social animal is central to the *Bildungsroman,* as it, in part, traces the development of the protagonist as a social being; protagonists become representative symbolic reflections of different socio-economic circumstances, and as such, George Lukács has argued, "their individual existence cannot be distinguished from their social and historical environment. Their human significance, their specific individuality cannot be separated from the context in which they were created" (1964, 19).

The protagonist's experience of the social and cultural environment depends on several interrelated factors such as gender, race, ethnicity, and class, because these determine the individuals' position vis-à-vis the social context. If we examine *Bildungsromane* of different periods and social circumstances—for instance *The Awakening* (1899) by Kate Chopin, *Look Homeward, Angel* (1929) by Thomas Wolfe, *Daughter of Earth* (1929) by Agnes Smedley, *The Catcher in the Rye* (1951) by J. D. Salinger, *Brown Girl, Brownstone* (1959) by Paule Marshall, *Pocho* (1959) by José Antonio Villarreal, and *Delia's Song* (1988) by Lucha Corpi—we find not only distinct *Bildungs* experiences in respect to era and social context but also the crucial determinant of gender in the protagonist's *Bildungs* process. The interplay of tensions between the individual protagonist and his or her social and cultural environment shifts with history: in looking at the development of the *Bildungsroman,* we thus encounter, for instance, changes that have taken place in self-development reflected in this literary form, changes extending from a male-defined, eighteenth-century concept of *Bildung* to contemporary female perspectives on identity and self-definition.[2]

The *Bildungsroman* emerged within the particular social and intellectual context of eighteenth-century Germany and has traditionally been defined as the somewhat autobiographical novel of formation, portraying a young man's development from innocence and ignorance to maturity and knowledge. Critical studies of the *Bildungsroman* invariably go back to Goethe's *Wilhelm Meisters Lehrjahre* (1795–96), the prototype of the genre, which originated the paradigm of the *Bildungsheld:* "A young male hero discovers himself and his social role through the experiences of love, friendship, and the hard realities of life," as described by one of its earliest critics, Wilhelm Dilthey (from Cocalis, 399). This development was based on the eighteenth-century German notion of *Bildung*, the gradual development of the protagonist toward a specific *Bildungsideal* of the German *Bürgertum*. Thomas Mann defines this ideal as "inwardness, the culture [*Bildung*] of a German implies introspectiveness; an individualistic cultural conscience; consideration for careful tending, the shaping, deepening, and perfecting of one's own personality or, in religious terms, for the salvation and justification of one's own life" (from Bruford, vii). This "tending" and "shaping," "deepening" and "perfecting" of the hero's personality, his inner being, constitutes the very essence of the traditional *Bildungsroman*.

In his criticism of the genre, Wilhelm Dilthey describes this process of formation as a continuous, chronological movement toward wholeness:

> The *Bildungsroman* examines a regular course of development in the life of the individual; each of its stages has its own value and each is at the same time the basis of a higher stage. The dissonance and conflicts of life appear as the necessary transit points of the individual on his way to maturity and harmony. (from Tennyson, 136)

However, in the traditional *Bildungsroman* the hero's growth process usually culminates with his accommodation to the social order; the protagonist becomes a burgher with bourgeois values, or as Hegel succinctly describes the classical *Bildungsheld:*

> Especially young men are these new knights who have to make their way, and who regard it as a misfortune that there are in any shape or form such things as family, bourgeois

society. . . . It is their aim to punch a hole in this order of
things, to change the world. . . . These struggles are, however,
in the modern world nothing but the apprenticeship, the
education of the individual at the hands of a given reality. . . .
For the conclusion of such an apprenticeship usually
amounts to the hero getting the corners knocked off him. . . .
In the last analysis he usually gets his girl and some kind of
job, marries and becomes a philistine just like the others.
(from Swales, 1978, 20)

According to Hegel the protagonist of the *Bildungsroman* exchanges
youthful optimism for conventional resignation; his *Bildung,* his path
to maturity and wholeness, steers him toward an acquiescence to
existing social values and norms. The tensions between self and society, between inner needs and outer expectations, are solved
through conformity and a recognition of the "validity of the established order" (Scholl, 7), emphasizing the conservative nature of the
Goethean model.

Since *Bildung* is a historical concept subject to historical shifts in
sensitivity and values, the general thrust of the *Bildung,* as it is portrayed in the *Bildungsroman,* undergoes a perpetual process of transformation. As Susan L. Cocalis documents in her study "The Transformation of *Bildung* from an Image to an Ideal," at the time of
Goethe the concept had already changed from its original meaning,
reflecting historical and philosophical changes taking place during
the seventeenth and eighteenth centuries, and the abstract nature
of the concept has continued transmuting with the times ever since.
This meant a departure from the idealism and social conservatism
of the German *Bildungsroman* and a continuous transformation of
the concept. These changes were characterized by radical inversions
and repeated rejection of traditional values and ideals, thus illus-
trating the dialectical nature of the genre. As the *Bildungsroman* was
adapted to other national literatures, it took on characteristics pe-
culiar to time and place and brought about significant expansions
of the genre and the concept of *Bildung* to accommodate other cul-

tural and historical variables to the German model. During the twentieth century, for example, the process of development has been increasingly characterized by disillusionment and confrontation with a hostile environment; the possibility of developing a harmonious and coherent self within the social context may be questioned; uncertainties of contemporary life are reflected in the often indeterminate endings of the modern *Bildungsroman,* in which social integration is only obtained through some kind of compromise.

With the changing concepts of *Bildung* and the expanded definition of the genre, the image of the *Bildungsheld* has undergone a process of transformation as well; as R. W. B. Lewis points out, "Every age of fiction develops its own representative hero: its own human image of the values it acknowledges and the force or power it respects and responds to" (31). Critic David H. Miles sees in these changes the transformation of the *Bildungsheld* as "picaro" into the "confessor": "The novelist no longer wandered down life's road with his magic mirror, but returned it to his cell, where he hung it directly above the writing desk, to catch every distortion of the world as mirrored first in his own consciousness" (1974, 989). This internalization of the *Bildungs* process came to be characterized by an increasing sense of alienation from the surroundings. Evoked mainly by sociological and psychological factors of contemporary reality, the theme of alienation has developed to such a degree in the male-authored *Bildungsroman* during the twentieth century that the possibility or idea of any true *Bildung* is questioned or parodied; the most extreme example of this trend is perhaps Günter Grass's *Die Blechtrommel,* a parodic tale of a dwarf whose most remarkable growth is purely phallic. Some critics, such as Miles and Sammons, see this development as a sign of the very end of the genre, not taking into account that they are considering novels dealing with the *Bildung* of white males only.

In contemporary American literature, however, the *Bildungsroman* has in fact become one of the most viable literary forms in women's and minority literature; as Bonnie Hoover Braendlin points out, *Bildungsromane* written by societal outsiders, men and women of marginal groups, portray "the particular identity and adjustment problems of people whose sex or color renders them unacceptable to the dominant society; it expresses their struggle for individuation . . . an identity defined by the outsiders themselves or by their own cultures" (1983, 75). Chicano literature is a good example of this trend. Some of the first Chicano novels to be published were *Bildungsromane*, for example, *Pocho* (1959) by José Antonio Villarreal, *. . . y no se lo tragó la tierra* (1971) by Tomás Rivera, *Bless Me, Ultima* (1972) by Rudolfo Anaya, works that to a great extent focus on the question of Chicano cultural and social identity. Likewise, and the subject of this study, the majority of the Chicana novels published to date center on the particular challenges the *Bildungs* process presents to the individual Chicana in her struggle for a self-defined identity. Their contribution of new social and cultural perspectives on the process of individuation confirms the continuous viability and transformation of the genre.[3]

Despite developments in the concepts of *Bildung* and a changing image of the *Bildungsheld,* some features remained staple elements of the genre, and the basic definition also remained virtually the same. Until recently the definition of the *Bildungsroman* rested upon certain thematic features, which Barbara A. White sums up as follows: "The hero rejects the constraints of home, sets out on a journey through the world, obtains guides who represent different world views, . . . and meets with many setbacks before choosing the proper philosophy, mate and vocation" (3). To these principal characteristics Jerome H. Buckley adds experiences that involve "at least two love affairs or sexual encounters, one debasing, one exalting, and demands that in this respect and others the hero appraise his values" (17). It becomes clear that the defining characteristics of the genre presupposed male prerogatives.

In his study on the German *Bildungsroman,* Martin Swales suggests that the genre intimates "an inalienable need in man to have a story, to know himself as part of that linear flow of experience which cannot be halted at will" (32). Most male critics of the genre seem to concur in that they perceive, define, and analyze the *Bildungsroman* from a male-centered perspective. For example, Lothar Köhn's meticulous study of the genre, "Entwicklungs- und Bildungsroman: Ein Forschungsbericht" (1968), assumes that the *Bildungsroman* deals with the development and formation of a young man, reflecting male education and experiences. In *Season of Youth: The Bildungsroman from Dickens to Golding* (1974) by Jerome H. Buckley, the genre is defined throughout in male terms: the author underlines this assumption in his concluding assertion that the child protagonist with his questioning sense is father of the understanding man (282). A similar perception characterizes François Jost's approach in a comparative study of the genre; accordingly, the *Bildungsroman* portrays "the first years of manhood" when the young man educates himself and "recognizes his place in the world; he begins to distinguish, to be able to define this man who is himself" (137). These defining characteristics are only reiterated in the most recent study, *The Apprenticeship Novel* (1984) by Randolph P. Shaffner. The author claims to attempt "a functional definition" (ix) of the genre, yet in his explication of its fundamental principles he neither questions nor modifies previous definitions: the *Bildungsroman* is still the story of a young hero who at the conclusion "has usually already become . . . a man" (25).

If we turn to studies on the artistic variant of the genre, the *Künstlerroman,* we encounter similar male-centered perspectives. In one of the few book-length studies on the *Künstlerroman, Ivory Towers and Sacred Founts* (1964), Maurice Beebe thus defines the artistic version of the *Bildungsroman* exclusively as "the story of a sensitive young man," the male writer's fictional self-portrait (4). The basic contention of the study is emphasized when the author argues that "every artist is a man" (313), who, although he might be destroyed in the process, "must go to Woman in order to create" (18). Beebe's portrayal of the representative protagonists of the *Künstlerroman* as sensitive young men of artistic temperament who struggle against "the possible fates of the woman-trapped artist" (280), yet need women for creative purposes, is indicative of the general portrayal of women as the necessary "other" of the traditional *Bildungsroman.*

The majority of these purportedly general studies of the genre focus entirely on *Bildungsromane* written by males; the critics theorize about the universality of the individual process of development and growth toward maturity and independence, yet give almost exclusively male examples of typical developmental patterns.[4] The outcome is a definition of the genre that applies only to male experiences. Many of these studies take into account that *Bildung* is a relative concept, influenced by many interrelated factors such as historical period, cultural context, and economic circumstances, but neglect to recognize that the question of gender may radically change the very process of self-development and thus also the definition of the *Bildungsroman* itself.

This androcentric approach to the *Bildungsroman* is a good example of what Elaine Showalter calls male critical theory, "a concept of creativity, literary history, or literary interpretation based entirely on male experiences and put forward as universal" (1981, 183). One of the main objectives of feminist criticism during the last two decades has been to challenge this "dog-eared myth of intellectual neutrality" (Kolodny, 163), and expose the misogyny of literary practices in the general subordination of women in literature and the exclusion of women from literary history.

Feminist criticism of the *Bildungsroman* follows two general trends in feminist literary criticism, the dual task of "looking at the sins and errors of the past" and revealing the "grace of imagination"

(Heilbrun, 1975, 64) of women's literature. The former critical approach sets out to unmask the stereotyped images of women in male literature and the critical neglect of women's writings in general; the latter approach endeavors to unearth women writers and the literary traditions they represent. Feminist critics are asking new and different questions of literature and follow to a great extent what Adrienne Rich has proposed as the common objective of such criticism:

> A radical critique of literature, feminist in its impulse, would take the work first of all as a clue to how we live, how we have been living, how we have been led to imagine ourselves, how our language has trapped as well as liberated us, how the very act of naming has been till now a male prerogative, and how we can begin to see and name—and therefore live—afresh. (35)

An example of the first mode of criticism, and the only study to my knowledge on images of women in male-authored *Bildungsromane,* is Bonnie Hoover Braendlin's dissertation "*Bildung* and the Role of Women in the Edwardian *Bildungsroman.*" Her work, which studies exclusively British examples of the form, examines the secondary role of women characters in relation to the *Bildungsheld* and reveals certain male perceptions and attitudes toward the other sex and aspects of the general portrayal of women in the genre.

The period at the turn of the century was characterized by changes in cultural norms and values, in part as a reaction to the austerity of the Victorian past. At this time the Goethean principle of *das Ewig-Weibliche,* similar to the English "feminine ideal" and the American "cult of true womanhood," were confronted with new concepts of the liberated woman. Braendlin reveals that women were portrayed as the necessary "other" in the *Bildung* of a young man, a means to an end, so to speak, for the Edwardian *Bildungsheld.* The protagonist's confrontation with the seductive and destructive female temptress signifies an important passage in his process of development, but the goal of that process is to marry a modern embodiment of the Eternal Feminine, "that principle of unselfish love that compliments and fulfills male striving" (310). This portrayal of women as either sinners or saints is underscored when it comes to questions of women's independence and sexual freedom. Although the works under consideration reject the Victorian past in general, they still endorse the concept of "the maternal angel-goddess, guardian and perpetrator of inherited moral values" (311); women who try to free themselves from this social role are strongly condemned. Women's sexual freedom in itself is strongly condemned as well and only applauded in so far as the protagonist can benefit from this freedom: "All the young Edwardian heroes enjoy having their women freed . . . from sexual prohibitions, but only if those women conform to predetermined social roles" (321). Braendlin sees this development as one in which the principle of the "Eternal Feminine" becomes explicitly sexual and turns woman into the sexual "other" of the *Bildungsheld,* a process "that contributes to a conversion of Victorian paternalism into modern sexism" (321).

The images of women emerging from male-authored *Bildungsromane,* male constructs of selfless angels or selfish monsters, are representative of the general portrayal of women in literature and illustrate to some extent anthropologist Sherry Ortner's argument that woman has symbolically become the "embodiment of the mysterious and intransigent Otherness which culture confronts with worship or fear, love or loathing" (Ortner, 86). When we turn to the female *Bildungsroman* we find that the protagonist not only has to contend with this sense of "otherness," but must also deal with constricting social and cultural forces within her own particular environment in order to successfully complete her own process of self-development. Feminist criticism on women's *Bildungsromane* reveals not only "the grace of imagination" of this body of literature but also how the conditions for self-development are vastly different for women; the passage toward that goal must consequently vary from that of the male counterpart.[5]

An archetypal approach to women's novels of development is found in *Archetypal Patterns in Women's Fiction* (1981), in which Annis Pratt identifies the story of Apollo and Daphne to be one of the predominant paradigms in women's fiction. Repeated endlessly in similar stories, it has become a cultural archetype, "the rape-trauma archetype" (5) of women's experiences: "The tension between what Apollo intends and Daphne is willing to accept, between forces demanding our submissions and our rebellious assertions of personhood, characterizes far too much of our fiction to be incidental" (6). Given that the quest for identity is one of the classic themes of all times, Pratt sees these "undertones of the mythic" (13) as especially predominant in women's novels of development, yet with distinct characteristics distinguishing them from their male counterpart; as Pratt maintains elsewhere, "If there is a 'myth of the hero' there must also be a 'myth of the heroine,' a female as well as a male *bildungsroman,* parallel, perhaps, but by no means identical" (1971, 877). While the male quest for identity is socially and culturally sanctioned, social norms demand that women "grow down rather than up" (168). This, then, is the reason why women's quest for identity can only take place within a context of rebellion. Pratt identifies "the green-world archetype" (16) as a recurring pattern in female novels, representing freedom and independence for the young woman. This state of innocence, including visions of the ideal lover and erotic freedom, is disrupted through the intrusion of the "rape-trauma archetype" demanding submission to patriarchal norms.

The collision between the evolving self and the role society imposes upon women constitutes the recurring tension that runs through most of women's fiction. Societal requirements are antithetical to the true *Bildung* of the protagonist, producing what Pratt describes as the "growing-up-grotesque archetype" (29) in which the outcome of the development process is thwarted into an inversion of that process: it becomes clear, states Pratt, that in most novels of development growing up female is portrayed as "a choice between auxiliary or secondary personhood, sacrificial victimization, madness, and death" (36). The consistency of the pattern of conflict between the evolving self and patriarchal demands in women's fiction leads Pratt to conclude that "the patterns of pain in the female *bildungsroman* are embedded in image, leitmotif, and larger narrative patterns; their antitheses are images of desire for authentic selfhood" (16).

This finding is reiterated in another study, *Growing Up Female: Adolescent Girlhood in American Fiction* (1985) by Barbara White. Surveying over two hundred novels of female adolescence published between 1920 and 1972, White documents that there is a striking consistency in the way women authors have chosen to portray the female coming-of-age process:

> There is a constant sense of *deja vu* when girls envy their brothers, when they express outrage at being molested by a man, when they try to avoid housework, or when they say they feel enclosed, imprisoned, stuffed in a sack, or under a bell jar. In novel after novel the protagonist is in conflict over her gender identity. . . . In her rebellion against growing up female the adolescent heroine is usually besieged from within and without. She is hampered both by the strength of social institutions designed to prepare her for a subordinate role and by her own inner conflicts and passivity. (137)

This thematic consistency continues in female adolescent novels published from 1972 to 1982; although the feminist movement has had some effect, above all in the authors' frequent inclusion of sex, modern feminist consciousness, lesbianism, and other issues of the feminist movement, White finds that most of them resemble past novels of female adolescence and concludes that "substantial change in the fiction of female adolescence may have to await extensive social change; it is certainly revealing that contemporary novelists who try to present more positive images of growing up female have difficulty staying within the realistic tradition of the adolescent novel" (173). In this White concurs with Ellen Morgan's contention that as long as social reality remains firmly patriarchal a realistic novel about a liberated woman is "very nearly a contradiction in terms" (Morgan, 277).

This argument that female *Bildungsromane* can only come into existence when the possibility for a true female *Bildung* becomes a reality and the social and cultural environment accepts female independence and struggle for self-development is also the conclusion of a recent study, *The Myth of the Heroine: The Female Bildungsroman in the Twentieth Century* (1986) by Esther Kleinborn Labovitz. Taking the missing female heroine in the *Bildungsroman* genre as a point of departure, Labovitz points out that the exclusion of the female heroine from the *Bildungsroman* tradition was based on historical, social, and cultural facts, and she argues that "female heroines have been left out of the *Bildungsroman* not because of evil conspiracies of men in general, or male novelists in particular, but because the *Bildungsroman* was considered only in male terms" (245). Seeing many nineteenth-century female novels as stunted attempts at self-development, the "truncated female *Bildungsroman*" (6), Labovitz goes on to delineate the characteristic thematic features of the twentieth-century female novel of development. The recurring pattern of themes such as self-realization, sex roles, education, and attitudes toward marriage leads Labovitz to conclude that

> the female heroine's global response to patriarchal society determines the climate of the works considered here, influencing and coloring the heroine's quest in every stage of her development. To the degree that she can resolve her condition in that society, to that degree will she proceed with her quest. Until then, she is unable to determine her career plans, settle her marriage dilemma, or give herself an identity and a name. (251)

Labovitz does not tackle the question of whether a true female *Bildung* is at all possible within a patriarchal social order, a proposition very much doubted by White and Morgan, as previously mentioned, but sees the process of self-development rather as "the stages of learning how to live in the future" (257).

It becomes clear, then, that the thematic features of the female *Bildungsroman* deviate significantly from those of the male counterpart. If male *Bildung* is characterized by "the confrontation of the hero with his environment" (Shaffner, 8), an environment he may choose to oppose for existential reasons, this confrontation turns into rebellion when it comes to the female *Bildungs* hero, an essential and in many ways unique rebellion against social and cultural gender norms inimical to an independent and authentic female identity; as Pratt points out, "the hero does not *choose* a life to one side of society after conscious deliberation on the subject; rather, she is radically alienated by gender-role norms *from the very outset*" (36). Consequently, as "the expected sequence of life phases is disrupted at every step by the tension inherent in women's experience" (Pratt, 169), female *Bildung* can only take place under circumstances radically different from those of the male hero. The overt or subtle presence of patriarchy throughout women's literature becomes particularly pronounced in the female *Bildungsroman,* as it is within its confining conditions that the heroine has to pursue her quest for selfhood; for the female heroine coming into consciousness can only be "synonymous with her refusal to play the transcendent Other" (Lazzaro-Weis, 32), and in the process she must necessarily oppose the very norms which the male-defined tradition of the genre represents.

"Is there such a thing as a female *Bildungsroman*?" asks critic Carol Lazzaro-Weis in a recent article. "Probably not," she argues, "which is why it has been necessary over the years for many women writers and critics to invent one" (34). This point is well taken, as the female

Bildungsroman departs from the male-defined tradition in significant ways. Women writers have adopted the central idea of the genre, that is, conscious human self-development, to portray a new and different *Bildungs* process, corresponding to the different facets of female self-development; as Labovitz contends, "The *Bildungsroman* is no less a viable structure for the female heroine by virtue of her different developmental process, but rather as the vehicle advocating fuller exploration of women's goals and expectations allows for a re-defining of the genre" (8). By appropriating the genre for the female version of the *Bildungs* process, contemporary women writers challenge and expand its former thematic and formal definitions. As women are writing their own experience, confronting all-embracing questions concerning female identity and female education in the broadest sense of the term *Bildung,* they are "inventing" the female version of the *Bildungsroman.*

The recurring question of whether a true female *Bildung* is at all possible within a patriarchal social order, a proposition very much doubted by several feminist critics, is crucial for the understanding of the female *Bildungsroman,* yet may essentially be beyond the scope of the genre. Central to the female *Bildungsroman,* whether chronological or retrospective, is the exploration of the path toward self-development, the process of becoming, and as Pratt indicates, the resulting "potential for personal transformation" (178); the female protagonist becomes part of "an evolutionary spiral, moving from victimization to consciousness" (McDowell, 195) and emerges in the end with a heightened awareness of herself and her situation as a woman. The denouement of the *Bildungsroman,* a generally open-ended conclusion, only reveals her *potential* for forming her life in accordance with her own convictions and desires. Furthermore, critics Abel, Hirsch, and Langland argue that

a distinctive female "I" implies a distinctive value system and unorthodox developmental goals, defined in terms of community and empathy rather than achievement and autonomy. The fully realized and individuated self who caps the journey of the *Bildungsroman* may not represent the developmental goals of women, or of women characters. (10)

As these critics point out, although the traditional term *Bildung* has been adopted to indicate this developmental process, its implications are quite unorthodox when it comes to female characters. By depicting the female journey out of the "cramped confines of patriarchal space" (Showalter, 1981, 201), a notion that applies to the social as well as the literary sphere, women writers are transforming the very concept of *Bildung* and creating a female discourse based on distinctive female paradigms of self-development.[6]

The intimate connection between the quest for self-development, a sine qua non of the female *Bildungsroman,* and the concept of creativity as a catalyst for self-discovery is the basic theme of many female *Künstlerromane*. However, "to be a creative woman in a gender polarized culture is to be a divided self" (Ostriker, 1985, 60). The female artist has to contend with not only confining social and cultural definitions of her role as a woman, but also with the very concept of herself as an artist. Down through the ages creativity has been defined in exclusively male terms, and Gerard Manley Hopkins's assertion that "the male quality is the creative gift . . . [which] especially marks off men from women" (from Gilbert and Gubar, 3) is not an anomaly, but rather underscores the heretofore general assumption. Literary men, writers and critics alike, have concurred in their definition of the poet as "a man speaking to men" (Wordsworth, 937) and the storyteller, who "in every case. . . is a man" (Benjamin, 86), as speaking to "the younger men in his audience" (N. Frye, 1973, 164). The male primacy in the creative realm has been reinforced in religion and myths where the creator is always male, but as Susan Gubar points out, "the creation itself is the female, who, like Pygmalion's ivory girl, has no name or identity or voice of her own"; the very fact that until recently "women have been barred from art schools as students yet have always been accepted as models" (293) emphasizes the exclusion of women from the creative sphere. The depiction of the male as the creator and the female as the object for creation is a recurrent pattern in myths; consequently the quest of self through the creative act has been projected through male artists identifying with mythic male figures, yet accepted as manifestations of the universal patterns of this quest. The female *Künstlerroman,* written by and about women, thus operates "under the psychological and sociological burdens of a patriarchal society and its myths," as Grace Stewart points out in her study *A New Mythos: The Novel of the Artist as Heroine 1877–1977* (1979, 9). Myths generally reflect crucial periods in human life, and because the quest for self carries mythic undertones, Stewart has taken an archetypal approach to the question of female struggle for artistic self-fulfillment. Analyzing myths such as that of Faust and Demeter/Persephone and their relationship to the female artist as heroine, Stewart concludes that the female artist has to struggle with "a patriarchal heritage of myths that seduce them into playing other roles" (180). Her roles as a woman and as an artist are defined as mutually exclusive in these patriarchal myths, a reason why a new mythos is needed to guide the female artist toward personal and artistic fulfillment; each female *Künstlerroman,* believes Stewart, "will foster the growth of a new *Mythos,* a new base for the female artist" (180).

Since the conditions for development for the female artist are so vastly different from her male counterpart, female *Künstlerromane* build on their own traditions and developments. Linda Huf's study, *A Portrait of the Artist as a Young Woman: The Writer as Heroine in American Literature* (1983), stands essentially as a response to Patricia Meyer Spacks's question, "Where is the female equivalent of *A Portrait of the Artist as a Young Man?*" (Spacks, 1975, 200). Huf argues that female artist novels are rare, yet the female *Künstlerroman* differs quite significantly from its male counterpart, despite previous universal definition of the genre. Certain recurring themes characterize the female *Künstlerroman,* such as the conflict between female conditioning and woman's role as an artist, a conflict growing out of "the practical impossibility of being both the selfless helpmeet and committed craftsman" (6). Men play an important role in these novels, not as male muses, however, but rather as impediments in their artistic strivings. While the male artist contends with bourgeois conventionalism, the opposition to the female artist is all encompassing:

> [T]he artist heroine who fights for the rights of woman
> against the wrongs of man invariably discovers that The
> Enemy has outposts in her own head. She learns that she has
> inner foes as formidable as outer ones. Because she has
> internalized society's devaluation of herself and her abilities,
> she must slay enemies within her own ranks: fear, self-doubt,
> guilt. (11)

However, Huf finds that women of the last two decades have begun to overcome the guilt for creating; artist heroines have become more self-assertive in their stance against confining traditions and are increasingly "daring to be selfish" (157) in their strivings toward artistic fulfillment.

Thus before creative self-assertion is possible, woman has to come to terms with not only cultural and social constraints, but also a heritage of patriarchal myths and assumptions about herself as a woman and an artist. In addition to their exclusion from the creative realm, from the Christian myth of God, the father and creator of the universe, the religious paradigm of male creative power, to Harold Bloom's view of literary history as a series of filial relationships, literary women have to confront notions of having been "created by, from, and for men, the children of male brains, ribs, and ingenuity" (Gilbert and Gubar, 12). Adrienne Rich sees the re-visioning of this cultural history as an act of survival for women writers: "Until we can understand the assumptions in which we are drenched we cannot know ourselves" (Rich, 35); understanding the discrepancies between what woman is and what she is supposed to be is thus essential to the process of self-development.

In re-visioning the *Bildungsroman* tradition before approaching the Chicana *Bildungsroman,* it is worth recalling Goethe's vision of *das Ewig-Weibliche,* the Eternal Feminine, his ideal woman: "She is an ideal, a model of selflessness and purity of heart. She . . . leads a life of almost pure contemplation. . . a life without external events— a life whose story cannot be told as there is no story" (Eichner, 616). This image of a selfless woman, a woman without an authentic self, one who has no story, exemplifies the image of women as empty vessels, void of creative powers; as Gilbert and Gubar point out in *The Madwoman in the Attic,* "women have been told that their art . . . is an art of silence" (43). Women's *Bildungsromane,* identified by Ellen Morgan as "the most salient form for literature influenced by neo-feminism" (274), represent the process of un-learning the art of silence.

As we turn to the subject of this study, the Chicana *Bildungsroman* and *Künstlerroman,* this notion of breaking the silence becomes particularly apt because Chicana writers have only emerged in substantial numbers during the last two decades. For the Chicana, twice a minority, the silence has been especially deep: constricted simultaneously by patriarchal cultures and the dominant culture's stereotypes of her Chicana identity, the Chicana has been defined and confined within the mother/virgin/whore stereotypes of the past, both within her own Chicano culture and the larger American cultural context; much like Goethe's vision of the selfless woman, Chicanas were perceived to live a life "whose story cannot be told as there is no story." Thus, much of the literature on the Chicana—scant as it is—devotes its efforts "to the study of *what* the Chicana is and not *who* she is" and depict the Chicana only in relation to her socio-cultural role; as Campos Carr contends, "Few studies and impressionistic essays . . . center on the identity of the Chicana and how she views herself" (272).

Excluded from the canon of literature and misrepresented within it, the Chicana has remained an all-pervading absence in considerations of American literature, including feminist criticism devoted to women's literature in general. As an increasing number of women of color are beginning to point out, feminist literary criticism has been conducted predominantly by white women who have exercised "the same exclusive practices they so vehemently decried in white male scholars" (McDowell, 186). Among the most glaring examples of these exclusive tendencies of feminist criticism is Patricia Meyer Spacks's introductory comment to *The Female Imagination*—that as a white woman she is "reluctant and unable" (6) to construct theories about experiences she has not had, while she at the same time includes writers such as Isak Dinesen in her study. The effect of such critical practices is not only that white women's experiences become normative, but also that by using the gender term comprehensively, that is, "female imagination" or "women's literature," critics exclude any notion of other factors such as race and class that are relevant to the definition and comprehension of women's literature. As white feminist scholars are developing the idea of a female literary tradition, certain components of "women's" literature are still mainly unacknowledged. Thus Chicana authors, like many other women writers of color, have remained "beneath consideration, invisible, unknown" (B. Smith, 4).

Criticism on the female *Bildungsroman* or *Künstlerroman* follows these exclusive tendencies and contains hardly any references to ethnic women writers; in much the same way that male critics have neglected to recognize how the question of gender may radically change the very process of self-development, so feminist scholars have failed to recognize how ethnic variations of the developmental process may influence the underlying concepts of the genre.[7] Yet the ethnic context is a crucial component of the developmental process. It is through the interactions with the social and cultural environment, and therefore also with the traditions of her ethnic heritage, that the Chicana *Bildungsheld* gains an understanding of her individual self as a woman and as a Chicana. It is this duality in Chicana writings that critic Alvina E. Quintana has recognized:

> Women's literature provides the method, the voices, experiences, and rituals involved in growing up female. Chicana writers, like ethnographers, focus on microcosms within a culture, unpacking rituals in the context of inherited symbolic and social structures of subjugation. These writers are acting as their own ethnographers, using the word for self-representation. (1985, 12)

When we turn to the Chicana narratives of the last two decades, we discover that Chicana writers have used the *Bildungsroman* genre as vehicle for such self-representation. By placing the Chicana self at the center of their literary discourse and by tracing the development of complex and multidimensional Chicana characters, these writers explore who she is and how she came to be that way. Particularly interesting to this study is the emergence of a Chicana *Bildungsheld* who defies both Anglo and Chicano definitions of herself and who defines herself in opposition to "inherited symbolic and social structures of subjugation" (Quintana, 1985, 12) in her search for an individuality that is centered in the Chicano community.

The Chicana *Bildungsromane* chosen for this study are written in English and include *Victuum* (1976) by Isabella Ríos, *The House on Mango Street* (1985) by Sandra Cisneros, *Trini* (1986) by Estela Portillo Trambley, and *The Last of the Menu Girls* (1986) by Denise Chávez.

These narratives of Chicana self-discovery and self-definition reveal a diversity of distinct developmental experiences that calls for a diversified critical approach. I have therefore chosen not to impose upon these novels a series of predetermined themes, but rather to examine each novel individually with the purpose of illuminating some of the patterns of experience characterizing the Chicana process of self-development. The following chapters will place the Chicana *Bildungsroman* and *Künstlerroman* in an interpretive framework of the *Bildungsroman* tradition in order to illuminate and analyze the individual works and how Chicana authors are portraying the Chicana *Bildungs* process, while at the same time indicating how these works contribute to the very transformation of the genre. Questions such as how the Chicana writer explores the simultaneous experience of gender, ethnicity, and class and its effect on the Chicana developmental process, or how the concept of discovery of self in some cases is connected with the process of creation play a central role in this analysis of Chicana *Bildung*. Finding a general correspondence in themes between individual works, however, and believing a broad thematic arrangement of this study to be more meaningful than a strictly chronological one, I have organized this analysis of the Chicana *Bildungsroman* into two parts: Part One, "*Bildung* as Entrapment," examines *Victuum* and *Trini* as portraits of a female *Bildungs* process that leads to socio-cultural enclosure, while the ensuing mid-life awakening offers a vision of a potential personal transformation; Part Two, "*Bildung* as a Subversive Act," examines *The House on Mango Street* and *The Last of the Menu Girls* for their exploration of female development as reflected by the growing female consciousness and creative awareness of the narrating "I." While each individual novel portrays a distinct Chicana process of self-development, this body of Chicana *Bildungsromane* presents an interesting medium for understanding the development in Chicana feminist consciousness during a period of approximately ten years.

From *Victuum* to *The Last of the Menu Girls,* the Chicana *Bildungs-roman* portrays the process leading to selfhood and creative self-assertion with an increasing awareness and assertion of Chicana authenticity; in the process these novels expand our own concepts of female self-development.

PART I
BILDUNG AS ENTRAPMENT

Women often live out inauthentic stories provided by a culture they did not create. The story most commonly told to young girls is the romantic story of falling in love and living happily ever after. As they grow older some women seek to replace that story with one of free and independent womanhood.

—CAROL CHRIST

The general intention behind the traditional *Bildungsroman* is to render a realistic depiction of human self-development. In male *Bildungsromane* we thus find a close correspondence between, on the one hand, traditional cultural values and social gender role expectations, and on the other, fictional *Bildungs* representation. Since the patriarchal socio-cultural ideology favors the achievement of a male-defined identity, for the male *Bildungsheld,* the successful completion of the *Bildungs* process is also a confirmation of autonomy and manhood. Realistic representations of the male *Bildungs* process reveal what Joanne Frye identifies as a general "assumption of male autonomy" (4), and while the traditional goal of this process is an "accommodation to the modern world" (Buckley, 17), such accommodation does not threaten the protagonist's autonomy nor his perception of his own manhood. When we turn to the female *Bildungsroman,* however, it soon becomes clear that a realistic representation of the female *Bildungs* process, which follows the traditional pattern of portraying individual accommodation to socio-cultural values and gender role expectations, can only portray a female *Bildungsheld* who succumbs to social and cultural norms of womanhood, norms that are antithetical to an autonomous and self-defined female identity. Thus, when women authors unquestioningly follow the realistic premises of the traditional *Bildungsroman* the female protagonist will most likely, as Joanne Frye argues, "succumb to the femininity text" and "grow into the enclosing grid of the known social expectations" (78).

Whether we call it the "femininity text" as Frye does, the "Love Story plot" (Russ, 9), or the "social romance" (Langland, 113), these are literary plot conventions of a tradition of "patriarchal poetics" (Gilbert and Gubar, 72) that invariably confine women characters to either passive domesticity, that is, marriage and maternity, or madness and death. These plot expectations inform our literary heritage and present a dilemma to the female *Bildungsroman*, which sets out with the traditional *Bildungsroman* paradigm to represent female development within a patriarchal socio-cultural context, while at the same time trying to circumvent that same cultural ideology and corresponding plot expectations that confine the female *Bildungsheld* to a prescriptive and externally defined womanhood.

This dilemma of cultural expectations that underlie plot expectations versus the representation of a female *Bildung* forms the underlying tension of both *Victuum* by Isabella Ríos and *Trini* by Estela Portillo Trambley. These two Chicana *Bildungsromane* follow in part the traditional linear, chronological convention of the genre and portray a female *Bildungs* process that leads to marriage and maternity. In both novels, however, we encounter a resistance to this "narrative entrapment" (J. Frye, 6), a muted resistance, perhaps, that nevertheless leads the protagonists to seek an alternative *Bildungs* experience beyond socio-cultural norms of womanhood. Both novels seem to be the story of the exemplary "obedient daughter" (Moraga, 157), yet both novels struggle with the conventions of the male-defined *Bildungsroman* and the "ideological underpinnings of the erotic and familial plots" (J. Frye, 1). *Victuum* manifests a rejection of traditional narrative procedures and employs distinctive literary strategies for a Chicana *Bildungs* story; *Trini,* on the other hand, follows the narrative conventions of the genre, but tests in its plot structure the paradigm of the male quest story and demonstrates how the female quest story must diverge from that pattern. Most revealing in both novels, however, is the portrayal of a *Bildungs* process that leads the protagonist directly to domesticity and passivity, to socio-cultural/plot entrapment, and then later to an awakening to her self-effacing existence. This awakening leads both protagonists to seek authenticity and selfhood beyond the social confines of patriarchal structures.

1

VICTUUM

A Psychic Rite of Passage

When Sleeping Beauty wakes up she is almost fifty years old.

—MAXINE KUMIN

Victuum by Isabella Ríos is the first *Bildungsroman* to be published by a Chicana; it also holds the distinction of being the first copyrighted contemporary Chicana novel.[1] The implications of being a first, however, go far beyond mere bibliographical data, and the notion of Chicana writers breaking out of silence, therefore, takes on a unique significance as we approach this particular novel. It is also important to keep in mind that although what is generally referred to as Chicana literature is a relatively recent phenomenon that grew out of the Chicano Movement, this body of literature did not emerge from a cultural or literary void. Published in 1976, *Victuum* constitutes, both thematically and structurally, an important link between past traditions and Chicana narratives that have followed.

For centuries the oral tradition held a central place in the cultural activities of the Hispanic community, a tradition that passed on the history and heritage of the people as well as confronted the vicissitudes of their socio-political conditions.[2] While most female storytellers never made it to the printed page, the oral tradition is clearly present in the works of some early Hispanic women writers whose book-length narratives appeared in the 1930s through the 1950s. These include books such as *Old Spain in Our Southwest* (1936) by Nina Otero Warren, *The Good Life* (1949) and *We Fed Them Cactus* by Fabiola Cabeza de Baca (1954), and Cleofas Jaramillo's *Shadows of the Past* (1941) and *Romance of a Little Village Girl* (1955). The central concern of these personal accounts is clearly to remember and record the stories of the past, the loss of land, and with it the loss of a traditional way of life. "I lived in the land of storytelling," says Cabeza de Baca in *We Fed Them Cactus* (127), and like other women writers of the period, she builds on that tradition in her writing; incorporated into their stories of the past are stories by other storytellers, thus amplifying the oral quality of the texts.

These writers define themselves as Spanish, and their first-person narratives reflect a romantic nostalgia for the past; theirs are the stories of "the landed gentry, in whose veins ran the noble blood of ancestors who left the mother country, Spain, for the New World" (Cabeza de Baca, 53). These pastoral visions of the past and their ideological implications, indicative of what Raymond Paredes calls "a hacienda syndrome" (52), have made "some contemporary Chicano writers, interested in more political social commentary, shudder," as critic Tey Diana Rebolledo notes (98); however, despite their ideological and political shortcomings by contemporary Chicano criteria, these texts are Hispanic women's literary mediations of the ethnic consciousness of a particular time and place.

There is, however, very little concerning women in these texts, and women are only mentioned in passing in connection with their roles as mothers and wives. The writers do not seem to argue with the traditional role women occupy, but rather justify and accept it; yet despite themselves, perhaps, occasionally an ambivalence about social and cultural restrictions and feminine behavior surfaces in the text, as in this passage from *We Fed Them Cactus:*

> True to my aristocratic rearing, I had to lead a ladylike life
> and should not resemble that of our uncouth neighbors
> whose women were able to do men's work. I always envied
> any woman who could ride a bronco, but in my society it
> was not done. How skillfully they saddled a horse! I often
> watched them catch a pony out in the pasture, just as the
> men did on our range, but it never was my privilege to have
> to do it. (129)

It is obvious that Cabeza de Baca would have liked to have had the
freedom of her "uncouth" female neighbors, yet in keeping with the
times and her social status, she complied with the "ladylike life" she
had been conditioned to lead. The main concern of this early generation of Hispanic women writers was clearly not to explore the
Hispanic woman as subject of her own narrative text, but rather to
chronicle the history of her particular community, to remember and
revive the record of the past and a seemingly vanishing culture
through the art of storytelling.[3]

The generation of Hispanic women writers who emerged during
the early seventies, the Chicanas, were to differ decidedly from their
forerunners: gone is the romantic nostalgia of the early texts as
Chicana authors confront the social and political realities of the
present and grapple with who they are as women and Chicanas, that
is, members of an oppressed minority. Contrary to the submerged
presence of the feminine narrator in the earlier personal recollections of a male-dominated communal life, the Chicana emerges to
take center stage in the contemporary texts. Because early texts by
Hispanic women have remained largely inaccessible, Chicana writers cannot "easily lay claim to a past literature of their own" (Alarcón,
85); nonetheless there are cultural perspectives and traditions link-
ing present authors to their literary foremothers. Poised chronologi-
cally between the previous personal accounts by Hispanic women
and the unprecedented outpouring of Chicana fiction during the last
decade, *Victuum* represents an interesting transitional work and foreshadows in many ways the important generational shift in Chicana

narrative voice that was to take place during the 1980s: in its cultural perspective and a narrative construction that is based on voices speaking, it builds on past traditions; in its subject matter it points toward Chicana narratives that were to follow.[4]

Like many of the early personal reminiscences, *Victuum* is situated in a clearly defined temporal and spatial context. The novel takes place in Oxnard, California, and covers the life of Valentina Ballesternos over a period of approximately forty-five years, from 1925 to 1971. Part I constitutes the main body of the novel and covers Valentina's life from birth to marriage; Part II centers exclusively on her psychic experiences.

It is, however, both in form and content, an unusual *Bildungsroman*. Its subtitle, "A Classic Biographical Novel," seems to be an act of literary diversion on the part of the author, as neither holds true. By no stretch of the imagination is this a "classic" novel, nor does it fulfill our expectations in regard to a biography. This initial distraction is amplified as we enter the novel: except for the initial two pages, it is a novel of pure dialogue and technically, as critic Ramón Saldívar notes, "a tour de force in its almost total rejection of traditional narrative procedure" (1990, 176). As a means of conveying the essence of a Chicana *Bildung* the author employs literary strategies that counter our expectations. By rejecting the predominant literary standards of what Gilbert and Gubar call "patriarchal poetics" (72), Ríos indicates through its very structure the oppositional character of the text. This strategy of opposition also applies to the content of the novel: Ríos portrays the *Bildung* of Valentina Ballesternos from a female perspective, yet much is left unspoken in respect to the gender formation of this Chicana; by leaving unspoken what was basically unspeakable at the particular time and place of this novel, the author creates submerged meanings intrinsic to female development. She tells her story, but in a manner that

Bildung as Entrapment

brings to mind Emily Dickinson's famous advice: "Tell all the Truth but tell it slant—."

Victuum is, as mentioned earlier, a novel of pure dialogue, interrupted only on a few occasions by Valentina's stream of consciousness; there is no omniscient narrator, no narrative introduction, description, explication or commentary of any kind, only conversation. Ríos lets Valentina and the people of Oxnard, members of the so-called "silent minority," speak for themselves: through communal dialogues on daily events, historical anecdotes, and the effects of contemporary developments such as Prohibition, the Depression, and the beginning of World War II, a picture emerges of Valentina's social and cultural environment in the Chicano community. The novel thus becomes an invitation to the outsider, the reader, to enter Valentina's intimate world, the community of Oxnard, to witness the coming of age of one of its female members. The reader is drawn into the community and becomes an omnipresent listener to the conversations of family members, relatives, and members of the community that surround Valentina. Ríos thus spurns the rhetoric of fiction and uses instead the rhetoric of drama to make her characters and the community come alive before the eyes of the reader. By dramatizing Valentina's *Bildungs* process Ríos eliminates the role of the narrator—the traditional voice of authority—and brings the reader in direct contact with Valentina and her community.

This particular staging of the novel emphasizes the central role of the Chicano community in Valentina's *Bildungs* process. It also underscores Tomás Rivera's observation that "la comunidad es conversación; la comunidad es platicar" (1982, 12), that is, a cultural context that defines itself through the spoken word. Valentina relates to the community through conversations that, in turn, have a formative influence on her; the combination of internal and external speech, the interplay between her own stream of consciousness and the conversations she participates in or overhears, intimates that the process of self-development is achieved through an interplay between social and psychological forces, between her individual self and the communal world. Through this dramatic technique Ríos also reaffirms the oral tradition that is central to Chicano cultural heritage. "The folklore traditions are based on remembering, retelling, and reliving," Rivera argues (1979, 21)—the oral means of conserving and reconstructing strengthening elements from the ruins of a fragmented past. From a different perspective Richard Rodriguez contends that "the novel is not capable of dealing with Chicano experience adequately," precisely because of "their reliance on voice, the spoken word" (371). Given the importance of the spoken word in Chicano culture, it is perhaps not surprising, then, that Ríos adopts an unconventional dramatic style in her attempt to capture a Chicano communal context that is vital to the development of her Chicana protagonist. Through this particular staging of the novel Ríos indicates that Valentina's *Bildung* can only be seen from within the social and cultural context of the Chicano community, her individual self being intimately connected to the communal self.

In the introduction to the first issue of *Third Woman* (1981), "Hay Que Inventarnos/We Must Invent Ourselves," Norma Alarcón states that a creative approach to self must be central to Chicana writers in the process of "laying down the foundations of our self-definition as well as our self-invention" (6). This idea of self-creation is particularly pertinent as we turn to the content of the first novel to center on the *Bildung* of a Chicana. *Victuum* ventures into unexplored territory in Chicano fiction in portraying the process of Chicana self-development, a process of self-definition that involves what critic Bell Hooks calls moving from the margin to the center (ii). By portraying the *Bildungs* process of Valentina, the Chicana protagonist of *Victuum*, Ríos claims the Chicana "I" of literary discourse, an act of self-definition that challenges former literary exclusions and mis-

Bildung as Entrapment

representations; this is also a move into a new literary space that calls for means of expression appropriate to the act.

In "The Laugh of the Medusa" Hélène Cixous outlines what the objective of women's writing should be: "Woman must write her self: must write about women and bring women to writing. . . . Woman must put herself into the text—as into the world and into history—by her own movement" (245). For Chicana writers, twice distanced from literary traditions, this movement into the text becomes an act of self-creation poignantly captured in the initial sentence of *Victuum:* "I watch. I listen. For sound am I, silenced by the human ear at present; shaped matter unseen by the human eye at present" (1). In this opening scene we are tapping into the emerging consciousness of a Chicana still in a symbolic fetal stage. We are thus witnessing the coming into being of the Chicana literary persona, the literary "I," who "silenced" and "unseen," is in the process of appropriating the power of speech.

This Chicana consciousness about to be born possesses all the knowledge "gathered over centuries, epochs" (2), yet is aware that it will all

> slip back into the sleeping silence of my conscience, and as my tiresome, limp fingers fondle the outer sustenance, it will be decades before they'll possess the strength to pull from the depths of my brain the knowledge of yesteryears. All will be forgotten. I will cling close to instinct and intuition, and yet my tongue will lack the maneuverability to express all that I feel. (2)

While the Chicana has remained "silenced" and "unseen," the collective knowledge of her history has been doomed to a quiescent existence in the depths of her consciousness. This is the consciousness of the Chicana "Everywoman," and it becomes the task of the female hero, and a part of her *Bildung,* to retrieve and give voice to that knowledge.

Thus the initial two pages of *Victuum* center on this eternal process of creation and re-creation, the core from which the female voice will emerge. We enter alternately the consciousness of the mother and the fetus who are interconnected through the unending female cycle generating life, an interconnection that will form an important part of Valentina's *Bildung*. Through this initial focus Ríos indicates where the roots to a true female *Bildung* are to be found and that it is from the exclusive sphere of vital and essential female interdependency that the Chicana voice will emerge. If writing is to be an act of self-creation, as Alarcón and Cixous have suggested, then Ríos points to the very source of such self-creation.

It is significant that the opening scene in the first Chicana *Bildungsroman* is a scene of birth. This scene initiates a body of Chicana narratives on the quest for self-definition, a process of becoming often likened to the process of giving birth to self in language as Alma Villanueva indicates in her poem "I Sing to Myself":

> I/woman give birth:
> and this time to
> myself.

This concept of giving birth to self in language, the symbolic link between the concepts of the biological and the creative birthing, is further underscored by the author's (Diane López) adoption of the pen name Isabella Ríos, the maiden name of the protagonist's mother. By fusing the biological and the textual motherhood into one, the author becomes the symbolic "mother" who creates/births the Chicana literary "I."

With *Victuum* we enter the female sphere of the Chicano community; women take center stage as speaking subjects who through their general conversations share their lives and particular experiences with each other. This context of mutual female support and protection constitutes Valentina's environment as she grows up; apart from her immediate family, Isabella and Adolfo Ballesternos and their seven daughters and one son, Vallentina's numerous aunts and *comadres* hold great influence within the extended family structure and play a crucial part in Valentina's life during her formative years. This predominantly female environment exemplifies Nancy Chowdorow's observations on female sex-role learning, where "a girl is usually with her mother and other female relatives," forming part of an interpersonal web "that facilitates continuous and early role learning and emphasizes the mother-daughter identification and . . . affective relationships between women" (1974, 54). Thus it is within this stable female context that cultural and social values are passed on to Valentina; it is also within this context that Valentina's concepts of herself as a woman are formed.

The mother, Isabella, comes to play a pivotal role in Valentina's life. The symbolic gestatory symbiosis between mother and fetus continues after birth, only to be transformed into a psychic connection between mother and child. An Indian *curandera,* a semi-mythic figure from the past, is present at Valentina's birth and notices that she is born with a veil over her face, which according to Hispanic folk belief signifies that she will know the spiritual world. Isabella tells Valentina at a very early age that this spiritual ability they share must remain a secret between the two of them, thus creating a particular bond between mother and daughter. This bond will take on an extraordinary significance as Valentina grows into maturity.

Except for this psychic gift, however, the woman Isabella is hidden behind the traditional signs of "wife" and "mother," fulfilling the role she has been conditioned to play. It is a role she readily accepts and perpetuates as she educates her daughters in keeping with patriarchal doctrines of female behavior. Accordingly, she insists on her need for male authority and guidance, yet she continually proves herself quite a capable woman who, during her husband's frequent absences or frictions with the law, manages a large family. Likewise, after his death, she declares herself incapacitated: "What can I do? . . . I don't know anything . . . without Papa I'm lost . . . he took care of everything . . . he was the smart one. . . . He knew what to do always!" (153), yet she proves quite the contrary as she struggles to provide for her family. Despite her competence she continues to adhere to and perpetrate the patriarchal ideology of her dead husband; given the absence of a father, she deems it necessary to reinforce her daughters' deference to male authority.

Isabella's insistence on patriarchal values illustrates Karen Rowe's observation about the complicity of women within a patriarchal culture, "since as primary transmitters and models for female attitudes, mothers enforce their daughters' conformity" (243), a complicity, however, as Mary Daly points out, "that has in large measure been enforced by conditioning" (49). Having raised her daughters with the expectation that they will marry and be provided for, yet seeing their growing independence as they help the family economically, Isabella expresses bewilderment at the role they are taking on: "You shouldn't have to work. . . . How things change . . . you girls are brought up . . . for what?" (179).

This question stands unanswered; in her struggle to maintain the cultural mores and values of the family, she is caught between internalized patriarchal concepts of womanhood and the realities of her own life. Her daughters, trained in the ideology of submission, grow up to follow their mother's advice "to marry someone, who can provide for you . . . build you a lovely home, away from this environment . . . far away" (233), thus perpetuating their mother's allegiance to the traditional role of "wife" and "mother."

As she grows up Valentina becomes part of the extended female community of aunts and *comadres* who form an intimate part of each other's lives; through mutual support, emotional as well as economical, they form a women's network that sustains them on a daily basis. Through their conversations one becomes aware, however, that it is precisely here that many patriarchal values are transmitted and internalized. Throughout her childhood the aunts and *comadres* express their distress over Valentina's tomboyish behavior and their wish to "train" her so she may conform to their own concept of womanhood:

> "Oh, my child, look at you . . . you're still my barefooted eagle running leaping about without care, hair dangling every which way . . . so free and clever! I have always felt I must train you . . . tame you . . . make a lady out of you, because you have such potential. (172)

It is significant that to "train" Valentina properly, according to the aunt, is to "tame" her. To tame someone is to make someone tractable, in other words, easily managed and controlled, or to domesticate someone, that is, to train to live with and be of use to man. It is exactly this kind of training/taming the aunt has in mind: Valentina's so-called potential lies in developing similar characteristics:

> "Because a girl simply must grow up, to be a lady . . . feminine! . . . She has to be a good cook . . . believe me, that is one of the main things that keeps a husband happy. . . . I want the best for you . . . don't you see if you grow up to be a lady . . . a nice young lady . . .there's nothing a man won't do for you!" (59, 172)

Valentina's potential for future happiness depends on the degree to which she is able to please a man. These are the patriarchal definitions of womanhood that are transmitted to her as she grows up; with little in her surroundings to gainsay this definition of herself and her future as a woman, her development until marriage is a process of increasing self-denial.

The father, Adolfo, is, of course, one of the prime promoters of such "education" of Valentina. Although he is mostly absent from her daily life and dies while she is still young, he sets an example as the authoritarian protector of the family that is to shape her image of and relationship to her future husband. The central principle in

Adolfo's formation of his daughter is the control of her sexuality, underscoring the essential role controlled female sexuality plays in the preservation of patriarchal ideals:

> Surely I've been strict . . . especially with the girls . . . but a father must be with his girls . . . he must make sure they become young ladies goddesses for a man to worship . . . virgin princesses . . . you see mija, there's nothing more beautiful than the love between a man and a woman . . . and that love is freely expressed after marital vows. . . . Therefore young ladies must guard their intimate dark room, until commitments are made. . . . Keep your innocence. . . your virginity that is the gift a woman offers her husband on their wedding night!" (146)

Every aspect of Valentina's formation points to her future as wife and mother: she is to shape her life and control her body to the benefit of a future husband; she is to sacrifice herself, offer herself as a "gift" to please her future master.

Valentina's acceptance of patriarchal authority dictating her actions has its roots in her relationship with her father through which she has been taught to accept such authority. While Isabella exists as a constant nurturing maternal presence throughout Valentina's life, her relationship to her father is characterized by her dual image of him as a threatening authority and a protective father. When she is still a little girl she reveres her father: he is the gifted musician, the man of the world, the storyteller who brings exciting experiences to life with his stories of past adventures. Slowly, however, her larger-than-life image of him dwindles as she becomes conscious of his authoritarian ways, often reinforced with beatings. His attempt to have her older brother and sisters fulfill his own musical ambitions is often done by force, creating an atmosphere of paternal power to which Valentina reacts with fear. Having no special talents, she is outside his circle of attention, but when he on one occasion hears her sing and demands her to sing for him, her reaction and the ensuing contention between the two reveal much of the relational dynamics between father and daughter:

> "Yes sing . . . come on, child, sing! What's wrong with you! Sing!"
> "I-I-I can't Papa . . . I can't!"
> "I heard you with my own ears . . . Go on! What stops you?"
> "Papa I-I-I can't sing . . . I-I-I don't know music, really I don't!"
> "Don't be stubborn, Valentina!"
> "M-M-Mama it isn't that . . . I can't!
> "Quit crossing your eyes and stuttering! . . . There, take that, you stupid girl! . . . Quit crossing your eyes. . . . Stop crying! I didn't hit you hard! . . . Boy, what you need is some real slapping around . . . that would fix you. . . . Stop crossing them! . . . Did you hear me? . . . Don't you know they can get stuck? . . . And all that stuttering. . . . Ah! You just want attention . . . that's all you want is attention . . . go on, get out of here . . . go on, get out!" (86)

Rather than trying to please her father, here she attempts to remain outside his musical domain, thereby avoiding his continuous exertion of discipline and control.

She shows similar physical signs of fear in other situations with her father, but slowly, as she grows older, she accepts his authority and becomes more obedient. Her perceptions of him also change; after having experienced some of his defeats, including humiliating incidents with the police and some of his drinking buddies, and overhearing conversations about the difficulties he has gone through to keep the family together during some difficult times—"he's a sincere man; he's done the best possible" (64)—she comes to see his exertion of authority and control as an intrinsic part of his role as the benevolent patriarch of the family. Given this formation it is therefore not surprising that when she later accepts a marriage proposal, she also accepts the patriarchal authority her future husband immediately assumes as he forbids her to work so she can fulfill her role as his wife; Valentina, by then a trained beautician, consents to this prohibition.

Every aspect of Valentina's formation seems to lead up to her acceptance of marriage and a future role as a traditional "wife" and "mother." The image of marriage as a safe haven, transmitted to her as she matures, is closely related to the important influence the community of Oxnard has had on her development. Throughout her childhood her home and the extended family function largely as a protective bulwark against a threatening environment— the internal dangers of barrio life and the external, that is, Anglo, influences on their daily lives.

The Ballesternos family live on Meta Street, popularly known as the "Barbary Coast," a rough neighborhood with "putas across the street, gambling . . . cantinas . . . drunks in the alleys. . . you name it . . . this Barbary area has it!" Despite the poverty and crime that characterize this predominantly Chicano barrio, the family remains because Adolfo "believed in living among his people!" (234).

The pride in Chicano culture and language and a strong belief in the role of education that is instilled in Valentina from an early age stand in sharp contrast with her experiences at school: besides being subjected to deriding taunts such as "dirty Mexican," she is punished by her teachers for speaking Spanish. Because they utterly contradict and denigrate her cultural formation and her sense of identity, these experiences cause much bewilderment in Valentina. It is here that she becomes conscious that she will have to mediate between these two contradictory forces that form part of her life, a realization that is reinforced at home: "Those teachers . . . are gringos . . . . They have the superiority complex, and that is something the Mexican must face . . . but remember this always be proud . . . you are not lower than anyone else" (154); she will have to come to terms with Anglo attitudes toward her ethnic identity and, despite these, maintain pride in her ethnic roots.

Bildung as Entrapment

To counter the degradation Valentina faces in her daily encounters with Anglos, her aunts and *comadres* take great pains to impart the family history to Valentina in order to bolster her self-esteem and instill in her a pride in cultural heritage. It is from them that she learns about California's Hispanic past, when "the Ríos family had large spreads of land . . . orchards of oranges . . . lemons . . . you name it . . . cattle . . . large head of cattle . . . yes, we're ranchers from way back" (151). Through family anecdotes she becomes conscious of a proud Hispanic past that differs decidedly from their present situation. She also learns how her landowning ancestors were dispossessed and converted into a scorned minority in their own land: "Imagine . . . we owned parts of the county . . . Ventura County . . . and now like struggling fools we break our backs to buy what we once owned . . . only just a small part . . . so that we can grow some vegetables and fruit . . . and survive!" (151). These stories, contrasting past and present family fortunes, are permeated with a sense of loss, a loss caused by Anglos, which accentuates the present precarious economic situation of the Ríos's and the perpetual and omnipresent possibility of misfortune that informs their lives.

Valentina's experiences of social insecurity are further aggravated by the risks the barrio streets present to her as a woman. When she is still a little girl she tries to protect herself by cutting her eyelashes to avoid looking like "the clown women across the street," in other words, the prostitutes, and thereby avoid having men staring at her: "There, my eye lashes are gone . . . no trouble now . . . no stares from men . . . no nothing . . . it's all gone now" (39). This self-mutilation as a means of self-protection indicates the vulnerability she feels in the street, a vulnerability that is only aggravated as she grows older and experiences several incidents of attempted sexual violence: at one point she avoids the attacks of a man who breaks into her bedroom, only to have the police later accuse her of having enticed the man through provocative behavior; at another instance, a handsome

Anglo who wants to date her turns out to be a pimp who does his "shopping" in the barrio: "He cruises around; spots chicks . . . makes them like him . . . then he promises them marriage and carts them off to Los Angeles" (198), as one friend explains to Valentina. Clearly, the barrio experience is here portrayed from a female perspective: in addition to poverty and ethnic degradation, Valentina has to confront sexual harassments that accentuate her vulnerability in a male-dominated world and further increase the social insecurity of her daily life.

It is in this social and cultural context that the notion of *la casa*, that is, the home, the family, appears much like a safe haven that may alleviate some of the negative effects the environment has on the individual; it is here that ethnic pride and family solidarity are perpetuated as a much needed bulwark against racism and poverty. However, the concept of *la casa* as a "constant refuge" (Rivera, 1979, 22) does not always apply to the Chicana: it is often within the very confines of the home that violence is visited upon her, as is the case with both Valentina's mother and sister; the concept of the traditional family may perpetuate ethnic integrity and help bear the blows of oppression, but for the Chicana it may also be that very concept which perpetuates her oppression. These are the contradictions that inform Valentina's situation: her dual minority identity signifies that she will have to mediate between concurrent experiences of gender, race, and class oppression that mark her daily life, and this at a time and in a social context that does not offer any alternative to her present circumstances. Her seemingly inevitable drift toward marriage, following the advice to "marry someone, who can provide for you . . . build you a lovely home, away from this environment . . . far away" (233), therefore cannot be seen merely as her reaffirmation of Chicana values and cultural heritage, as Hoover Braendlin argues (83), but also, in the absence of an alternative choice, as her capitulation to the multiple oppression of her present circumstances.

Bildung as Entrapment

The first part of *Victuum,* which constitutes more than three-fourths of the novel, covers Valentina's coming of age, but ends abruptly with her acceptance of marriage. This lengthy first part may seem to be bogged down in "superfluous descriptions and innumerable humdrum occurrences" (42), as critic Francisco Lomelí points out, but it is exactly through these seemingly unimportant daily occurrences that we receive a detailed and multifaceted account of Valentina's development in its socio-cultural context. On the surface the conversations we overhear may seem rather irrelevant to her development, but slowly a female subtext emerges, revealing what Annis Pratt defines as "submerged meanings" (1981, 72) in the text: the representation of the triviality and insignificance of daily life is informed with meanings not always expressed; as Ramón Saldívar points out, "What remains unsaid is often as important as what is said" (1990, 179).

This lengthy and detailed account of Valentina's formation as a social being is thus replete with signs of the cumulative effect multiple oppressive forces have on her development; the traditional "taming" of a female adolescent that Valentina undergoes results in her gradual acceptance of patriarchal authority, and becomes an example of what Labovitz calls a "truncated female *Bildungsroman*" (6), or as Saldívar contends, the "story of her gradual victimization" (1990, 178). Being conditioned all through her childhood and adolescence to accept social and cultural norms of womanhood, Valentina acquiesces to the prescribed role of wife and mother as if this destiny is her only option in life.

It is significant that the first part of *Victuum* ends abruptly with Valentina's marriage. It is as if Ríos wants to indicate that this act terminates Valentina's social formation, particularly given the fact that the second part of the novel is devoted exclusively to her psychic experiences. Apart from letting us know that Valentina, like her mother before her, has eight children, the individual woman

Valentina disappears behind the sign of the traditional "wife" and "mother"; thereafter we are only given the content of her psychic experiences. Her psychic development in the second part of the novel thus stands in sharp contrast to the social *Bildung* that confines her to growing "down rather than up" (Pratt, 1981, 14), to socio-cultural entrapment rather than authentic female selfhood.

It is only through Valentina's psychic experiences that *Victuum* offers the potential for a possible *Bildungs* process; these experiences, being beyond patriarchal control, present the possibility of expanding and lending meaning to her own concept of self. Much as Valentina's social victimization is revealed through a submerged female subtext, so her psychic self leads a submerged existence throughout her life. While still a child, she is warned by her mother that the psychic gift she has inherited must remain a secret between mother and daughter: "Just don't tell anyone . . . no one . . . just tell me. . . . They will not understand . . . they'll call you crazy . . . they'll say you need to be put away . . . so listen to me . . . don't tell anyone!" (152). She is thus conditioned to grow up as a divided self: because of patriarchal definitions of reality, the psychic part of herself must remain hidden to avoid persecution; her later psychic development thus becomes, as critic Francisco Lomelí notes, "a search to become a whole person and somehow rid herself of the schizophrenic divisions" (1985, 42).

Through this hereditary gift Valentina becomes part of a submerged network of female contact, most notably between mother and daughter, but including other women in the family. This network presents an alternative approach to reality and knowledge, often serving as a female shield of protection, yet confined to secrecy: within the framework of patriarchal ideology, female spirituality is deemed evil, and a psychic woman may thus be accused of "being a witch or being crazy" or of having "devil-powers" (74). Throughout her adolescence she hears voices and has several premonitions of

Bildung as Entrapment

imminent threats to her own safety and that of others, but as she grows older these develop into elaborate dreams and visions of an extrasensory nature. These visions begin to appear after her father's death, yet it is her mother's death that becomes a sort of catalyst for Valentina's psychic development. Critic Judith Kegan Gardiner argues that since "relationships between mothers and daughters are central to the development of women's identities," a mother's death may prove crucial to the heroine's formation of her own identity (1978, 248). However, in contrast to Gardiner's contention that the death of the mother "becomes a death of childhood repression" (248), Valentina's dead mother becomes instrumental in Valentina's acceptance of her identity as a psychic; whereas she earlier had been intimidated by her own psychic powers, she learns to accept this part of herself when her mother becomes part of this extrasensory dimension of her life. The initial physical symbiosis between mother and fetus is thus transformed into an intimate psychic symbiosis, underscoring once again that it is through the sphere of inherited female psychic powers, and not in the patriarchal social sphere, that she may achieve an integrated sense of self.

Through her psychic powers, then, Valentina transcends the limitations conditioning her social world: through dreams and visions, she enters a psychic realm defined by the central principle that "the human being is indeed master of his own universe" (338), a revelation that contrasts dramatically with her social formation. This notion becomes catalytic to her psychic development: through numerous encounters with historic and mythic figures, she learns that "the human brain's capacity is infinite" (338), helping her to understand the infinite dimensions of her own psychic powers. The central purpose of these encounters is the knowledge these psychic representatives of different areas of human thought impart to Valentina. On one occasion she is taken on a long journey through time by one of her psychic guides for the purpose of teaching her about the human capacity for survival: "Human beings house the most powerful element on this earth . . . the human brain. The human being has survived in spite of the earth's beginnings and endings. This earth with its human inhabitants has had rebirths or reincarnations" (285). These notions of reincarnation and innate psychic access to knowledge reiterate the predictions made by Valentina's own fetal consciousness that the knowledge "gathered over centuries, epochs" would remain inaccessible to her conscious self until she gains "the strength to pull from the depths of her brain the knowledge of yesteryear" (2). As she reclaims this knowledge, it expands her sense of self and redefines patriarchal definitions of reality and truth. When Valentina begins to share her dreams and visions with her daughter Diana, we understand that she has come full circle in her development: by introducing her daughter into the psychic realm, much like her mother did with her, Valentina passes on a female heritage that nurtures her sense of self and her capacity for survival.

Interpreted from a psycho-mythological perspective, Valentina's psychic experiences may be understood as a psychic rite of passage, a possibility hinted at in a reminder she receives from one of her psychic guides: "Remember this, Valentina, all that you have envisioned are only dreams" (319). According to Joseph Campbell, "dreams are symptomatic of the dynamics of the psyche" (255). Valentina's dreams of her quest for knowledge may thus be interpreted as a descent "into the darkness . . . of her own spiritual labyrinth" (Campbell, 101), into the realm of the unconscious to pursue her quest for self-discovery and self-development. There she is confronted with the innate psychic powers she has had to hide and suppress, yet she recognizes that these "carry the keys that open the whole realm of the desired and feared adventure of the discovery of self" (Campbell, 8).

Whereas the first part of the novel portrays a linear external/social formation of the female protagonist, a formation that results in an increasing sense of alienation, the second part of the novel involves a vertical internal/psychic *Bildungs* process, what Annis Pratt terms a rebirth journey or a "depth journey into the psyche" (1973, 3); this second part of the novel takes Valentina beyond social boundaries, beyond patriarchal space, and centers upon the personal psychic sphere, her quest into her own unconscious for psychic wholeness. This division into an external and an internal quest for selfhood illustrates Carol Christ's distinction between the female "social quest," which more often than not leads to socio-cultural entrapment and alienation, and the "spiritual quest" through which a woman seeks to "integrate her self with herself" (1980, 8–12). We do not know, however, whether Valentina will be able to reach an integrated sense of self. As the novel abruptly ends Valentina remains in the psychic sphere without any indication of her seeking to reintegrate herself into the social sphere. Such descent into the psyche, Pratt observes, entails risks and psychological danger and is as likely "to lead to madness as to renewal" (1981, 142). *Victuum* leaves this question unresolved and presents only the potential for Valentina's successful completion of the psychic quest.

Victuum's subject matter and style allow for ambiguities in the interpretation of its meaning, yet it is possible that there is a clue to these ambiguities in its very title. The name comes from Valentina's last guide, Victuum, who takes her on a final journey to teach her a variety of subjects, ranging from theories of evolution and reincarnation to concepts of time and space. Critic Ramón Saldívar sees the title *Victuum* as a pun on the word *victim,* the trajectory of Valentina's life story as "the story of Valentina's victimization" (1990, 178), and her psychic experiences as a "flight to nowhere in the company of the symbolic Father" (1990, 180). *Victuum,* however, does not only pun on the word *victim;* it can also be interpreted as a slightly changed form of the Latin word *victum,* the accusative case of *victus,* which is the supine tense of *vincere*, to conquer; being a verbal noun, *victus* becomes equivalent to the English word *victor*, one who defeats or vanquishes an adversary, a winner; respectively, in the accusative case, *victum* can be translated as "to the winner." Thus the very title *Victuum* may present the riddle of the novel: is Valentina a victim or a victor? I argue that she is both. Valentina is an embodiment of the contradictions inherent in her experiences as a Chicana, a victim of multiple layers of oppression in her daily life and the limitations these place on her development as a woman. The novel, however, presents the potential of her redemption through a reclamation of psychic wholeness and her place in a psycho-mythic continuum that connects her to her past.

It is significant that the first Chicana *Bildungsroman* has an abrupt and ambiguous ending without clearly defined indications as to the direction the *Bildungs* experiences will lead the protagonist. After revealing Valentina's social conditioning within the confines of patriarchal ideology, Ríos introduces her into a psychic realm and has her undergo experiences that, much like a woman's spiritual quest, may "ground her in a new understanding of herself and her position in the world" (Christ, 1980, 9), yet the author does not reveal how these experiences may change her life or her concept of self. We can only guess at the implied significance of her psychic *Bildung*. *Victuum* takes the first step toward portraying a Chicana *Bildungs* process, yet Valentina's *Bildung* is perceived, as it were, "through a glass darkly" (Gilbert and Gubar, 17): whereas her social formation reveals an indirect critique of patriarchal ideology, her psychic *Bildung* becomes a vaguely defined quest for an expanded sense of self. This ambiguity about the realization of the *Bildungs* experience and the direction it may lead the protagonist in this first Chicana *Bildungsroman* may be interpreted as a symbolic reflection of the effects patriarchal conditioning has on a particular Chicana. How-

Bildung as Entrapment

ever, a more plausible interpretation of this vagueness is to see it as an expression of the author's artistic insecurities in respect to Chicana self-definition, what Gilbert and Gubar call an "anxiety of authorship," caused by having to "dance out of the looking glass of the male text" (71) to produce an independent and self-defined Chicana character.

An interesting extension of these textual ambiguities is the question of the very authorship of the novel. The actual author of *Victuum*, Diana López, writes under the pen name Isabella Ríos, the maiden name of Valentina's mother. The author thus uses the *Bildungsroman* both to express and camouflage herself: writing under the disguise of a pen name, she distances herself from her own text. Yet by adapting the name of the protagonist's mother, merging the biological and textual motherhood into one, she connects herself intimately to that same text. These subterfuges on the part of the author become another instance of an "anxiety of authorship" in asserting a Chicana literary identity, reinforcing the textual ambiguities in respect to a self-defined Chicana identity.

Victuum portrays, both directly and indirectly, a Chicana consciousness in the process of becoming, aware of the contradictions inherent in her experiences as a Chicana, yet still ambiguous about how to overcome these contradictions in order to envision and achieve a new definition of her Chicana self. The novel presents a sharp division between Valentina's external and internal reality, a formal representation of a divided self that underlines the need for an integrated sense of self. Her venture into a psychic sphere is a withdrawal from social boundaries in search of awareness and psychic wholeness, a quest that suggests only a potential path toward an authentic self in this first Chicana *Bildungsroman*.

2

TRINI

A Chicana Quest Myth

Female, a Quixote is no Quixote at all; told about a woman, the tale of being caught in a fantasy becomes the story of everyday life.

—RACHEL BROWNSTEIN

Trini (1986), by Estela Portillo Trambley, is perhaps the most conventional of the Chicana *Bildungsromane* under consideration in this study. Its narrative pattern is essentially chronological, showing a continuous development from childhood to maturity, much in keeping with the linear structural paradigm of the traditional male *Bildungsroman*. The story of the protagonist, Trini, is told in third person by an omniscient narrator and conforms to the convention of tracing the development through different stages of the heroic quest for identity, but with the essential differences social and cultural conditions generate in respect to female development. Like many narratives that cover the development from childhood to maturity, *Trini* carries, to use Annis Pratt's phrase, "the undertones of the mythic" (1981, 13). Employing the motif of the journey, an important element in quest myths, the author traces the *Bildungs* process of Trini, from her childhood in the Mexican valley of Bachotigori during the 1920s to the difficult migration north into the United States where in the early 1950s she is finally able to settle down in

57

Valverde, Texas. The narrative outline of *Trini* is structured around the basic patterns of the psycho-mythological "myth of the hero" as it has been outlined by Jung, Northrop Frye, and Joseph Campbell, but with the notable distinctions characterizing a female heroic quest. These deviations in heroic development illustrate Pratt's contention that "if there is a 'myth of the hero' there must be a 'myth of the heroine,' a female as well as a male *bildungsroman,* parallel, perhaps, but by no means identical" (1971, 877). In Trini's *Bildungs* process we perceive the broad outlines of the challenges and pitfalls of female development, that is, the developmental phases that form the basic pattern of "the myth of the heroine." *Trini* illustrates how the happy denouement of the traditional male *Bildungsroman* carries quite different consequences when it comes to the female quest for self. Being a Chicana *Bildungsroman* it reveals, furthermore, the additional hardships social and cultural circumstances present in the protagonist's *Bildungs* process.

In the prologue, Trini is confronted with a portrait of herself, a symbolic creation that she recognizes as her own image:

> The figure of Trini on canvas was painted into the light, almost as if it had appeared out of the depths of rocks and earth. The whole body was a movement of strength, sustained, yet free. There was something mystical about her eyes, dark, looking to the level of the living, yet seeing beyond. The hair flew loose and long in the wind. The most amazing thing in the painting were the feet, bare, brown, seeming to grow out of the earth itself. . . . Yes, thought Trini, it is me. What I am inside. . . . She had seen many women like herself, who had crossed a river illegally into the United States. So many brown women faceless in the world. Yet, here she was. Only she, a life etched in an unpoised moment, in a fragment of continuous change, all spelled out to its very beginning and all the beginnings to follow. (7)

Trini's recognition of her own being as strong and free, her life "spelled out to its very beginning and all the beginnings to follow," foreshadows the story of her *Bildungs* process, the stages in her life that have led up to this instance of self-recognition. The author's choice to introduce this *Bildungsroman* with a portrait of the Chicana *Bildungsheld* is significant because the German word *Bildung* was originally a synonym of *Bild,* that is, *imago* or portrait.[1] Because *Bild* translates as the artistic formation of a material into an exemplary model, the opening scene takes on a double meaning: Trini's portrait, much like the novel itself, becomes symbolic of an exemplary *Bild / Bildung* of one of "the many brown women faceless in the world" (7).

Another important aspect of this initial prologue is Trini's recognition of the portrait as an authentic reflection of herself. This points to a concern that formed part of the Chicano literary endeavors from the very beginning, namely the creation of authentic images reflecting the Chicano cultural and social identity. In the preface to the first Chicano anthology to be published, *El Espejo* (1969), the editors declared that "to know themselves, to know who they are, some need nothing more than to see their own reflection" (5). The Chicana, however, has until recently for the most part encountered only distorted reflections of herself. While contemporary Chicano literature has modified the predominantly negative image of the Chicana in Anglo-American fiction, she has with few exceptions been typecast into secondary roles with little attention to her individuality, her life as a Chicana. It is therefore not surprising that *Trini,* among the first Chicana novels to be published, is introduced by a supposedly authentic image of the protagonist, symbolic of the novelistic intent to create an authentic literary image of a Chicana.

Close ties to Mexico form an important part of Chicano cultural reality. The continuous migrations north across the Mexican-American border of 1848 reinforce these cultural ties and, at the same time, call attention to the geopolitical nature of the border. Thus several early works by Chicano authors use Mexico as the point of departure in order to render a literary depiction and interpretation of the migration north across the border into the United States and the social and cultural consequences of that migration.[2] This experience, however, was rendered from a male perspective without attention to the particular risks such migration may present to women. Given the fact that Chicanas "represent one of the most ignored and neglected groups of ethnic women in American society today" (Enríquez, 105), the women coming across the border from Mexico, *las indocumentadas,* have remained virtually invisible, the drama of their lives unacknowledged. In keeping with the general intent by Chicana authors to explore and articulate their identity as women of Mexican descent, *Trini* stands as a literary attempt to draw a symbolic portrait of one of the "faceless" *indocumentadas;* the experiences she confronts migrating north form part of her *Bildungs* process and shape her understanding of her individual self.

With *Trini* we enter into the world of Bachotigori, Mexico, a pastoral green valley, the archetypal Eden, poised in a seemingly timeless space. Shaped by indigenous beliefs, the mestizo community in the valley lives in harmonious coexistence with nature: "The people of the valley planted after the winds of February, everyone sharing the crops for miles around. No one person owned the land" (16). It is a world where the gods speak through the winds and the land is peopled by *duendes,* elf-like beings, and magic dwarfs who play with the children. This archetypal green world constitutes the microcosm of Trini's childhood.

Our initial introduction into this harmonious green world is accompanied by the death of Trini's mother. In light of *Trini* being a *Bildungsroman,* the death of the mother takes on special significance as it signals the disruption of Trini's social and emotional context and the initiation of the subsequent search for self. According to Nancy Chodorow a girl must model herself on her mother if she is to have "a strong, healthy, sex-appropriate identity" (60) within a particular social context. A fictional mother's death, then, indicates an absence of the maternal role model, which would insure the daughter of "an unencumbered ascent as a self-made person" (Gardiner, 1978, 244). The death of Trini's mother through a miscarriage, that is, as a victim of her own body and her biological social role, thus becomes a catalyst for Trini's own search for selfhood and a viable existence as a woman.

Sabochi, a young Tarahumara Indian, plays a central role throughout Trini's childhood; he is her guide into the natural and spiritual world, who makes "nature gods quite real" and speaks of the winds of "freedom, change, timelessness" (19). Through him she comes to recognize how closely she is connected to the valley, that "it is something in the blood," and that her sense of self is intimately related to "the love of the earth, the ways of the valley" (39), a vision of herself that will guide her throughout her life. This portrait of Trini as a free spirit at one with the green world coincides with Simone de Beauvoir's observation that the adolescent girl

> will devote a special love for Nature; still more than the adolescent boy, she worships it. Unconquered, inhuman, Nature subsumes most clearly the totality of what exists. The adolescent girl has not as yet acquired for her use any portion of the universal: hence it is her kingdom as a whole; when she takes possession of it, she also proudly takes possession of herself. (405)

It is in nature that Trini feels a sense of independence and wholeness. Her vision of herself as connected to a mystical natural sphere and her experiences of what has been termed "the green-world epiphany" (Pratt, 1981, 170) will in the course of her *Bildung* serve as touchstones in her quest for identity and selfhood.

As Trini grows into adolescence her feelings for Sabochi change: whereas before she had related to him as her playmate and a guide who could introduce her into the mysteries of life, she now sees him as a man who arouses "strange new magical feelings" (18) in her. Sabochi's departure becomes significant as it terminates their "chaste love" (N. Frye, 200) relationship and thereby also the innocent phase of Trini's life; her relationship to men will henceforth be of a different nature. Trini's first encounter with love in this green valley, reminiscent of the "prelapsarian mythic garden world where the male and female once existed as equals" (Goodman, 30), or of "the archetype of erotic innocence" (N. Frye, 200), forms an important part of her development, as it represents an independence she will slowly lose with her introduction into the norms of womanhood. This phase of Trini's development constitutes the green-world archetype of female development, the place "from which she sets forth and a memory to which she returns for renewal" (Pratt, 1981, 17), and it remains throughout her *Bildungs* process the ideal state of wholeness she tries to recapture in her quest for self.

Trini's discovery of this new emotional part of her being signals a turning point in her life, a moment when she no longer relates to the world as a child, but rather as a young woman:

> The rain was falling hard. Its excitement was her excitement. She opened her mouth to breathe in the wetness of the world, the discovery of herself, the greyness of the world empty of a Sabochi that would always be the thunder and lightning of her life. The excitement grew as if the world were opening up to strange, terrible things, with such beauty. (22)

These new sensations change Trini's perceptions of herself: as she becomes aware that "life was no longer a mere design of colors and dreams like the rainbow rocks" (29), she slowly withdraws from the world of her childhood. This emerging of a sensual being sends Trini to the mirror to contemplate her own reflection, finding "a trace of womanliness in the shape of mouth," yet still "a child's face, a face wanting so many things unhad" (34). Her glance into the mirror for her own self-image is a search for a viable self, a search for answers to who she is, and although her mirror image does not give her any

Bildung as Entrapment

answers about her self-identity, the traces of "womanliness" she finds in her still childlike face suggest that her transformation into a woman has begun.

These personal changes that Trini undergoes are paralleled and underscored by changes taking place in her social world, the harmonious green world of her childhood. The presence of foreign economic interests has violated indigenous sacred beliefs about the nature of gold and destroyed its significance to the communal identity and its relationship to nature. The presence of gold in the valley used to be a sign of a valley being "the sacred ground of Gods" (16), but now this sacred light has turned out to be "gold, only gold" (16), an indication that "the gods have left the valley" (17). This disruption of sacred beliefs, the breakdown of the previous harmony between the people, the land, and the spiritual world corresponds to the disruption of Trini's childhood, which causes a fragmentation of the wholeness she had experienced as a child in possession of herself.

Trini's departure from her childhood and its indigenous context is accompanied by her introduction to Catholicism. Tía Pancha becomes the prime purveyor of Catholic beliefs and introduces Christian concepts of human worthlessness into Trini's life; Trini is thus taught to think of herself as a sinner, "tainted and weak," who should be "meek and humble" (35), in perpetual need of forgiveness from an omnipotent God. Apart from challenging Trini's concept of herself as closely connected to the indigenous spiritual world, the aunt's Catholic doctrines also influence her budding perceptions of herself as a woman. She is admonished about "the importance of virginity," that "a girl must be very careful and remain unsullied up to her marriage day. She must go to her husband pure and dutiful" (95). Trini is made to understand her sexuality and the physiological changes she is undergoing in a patriarchal Christian context of physical prohibitions, rather than as part of the natural cycle of life. These

Catholic concepts of sexuality change her perception of herself and further remove her from the magic innocence of her childhood. Her previous freedom and independence in the natural world stand in sharp contrast to these new restrictions placed upon her life as she is about to enter womanhood. These changes make her "long for the old way of life" (38). She has reached a stage in her development when the adolescent girl, according to social conventions of female conditioning, "slowly buries her childhood, puts away the independent and imperious being that was she, and enters submissively upon adult existence" (de Beauvoir, 408). Trini's *Bildungs* process is thus informed by traditional female conditioning, which prepares her for her role as a woman within a patriarchal system but which also will have far-reaching consequences when it comes to her quest for selfhood.

The foreign economic exploitation of the valley and the consequent violation of its spiritual world is followed by a religious intrusion that transforms the individual perception of self and its relationship to the cosmos. This repetition of the colonization process eventually drives Trini and her family out of their green valley. The departure from the harmonious world of the valley is parallelled with Trini's adolescent awakening of self, her loss of innocence and her separation from the unconscious state of her childhood. This internal as well as external separation, what Pearson and Pope term "the exit from the garden" (68), exemplifies the initial stage of the heroic journey toward self-fulfillment, a central theme of mythic quest stories. According to Joseph Campbell, this mythic quest is a symbolic reflection of the *Bildungs* process: "The standard path of the mythological adventure of the hero is a magnification of the formula represented in the rites of passage, separation-initiation-return, which might be the nuclear unit, the monomyth" (30). These three principal stages of the monomyth, enacted through an infinite variety of incidents that represent the various phases of the quest story, constitute the mythical journey, initiated by a departure and culminating in a successful reconciliation. Trini's departure from the green valley of her childhood is the initiation of her journey that will become a spiritual and social quest for wholeness and an authentic female identity. Henceforth, driven by the central urge to recapture the lost harmony of her childhood, a proposition that may be defined as an "unconscious quest for the impossible" (Salazar Parr and Ramirez, 1985, 57), Trini undergoes trials and experiences that test her sense of self and mold her into a woman who must reconsider her own relationship to the world in order to realize her self.

With the departure from the pastoral green world, Trini sets out on a journey that presents extreme dangers from natural forces as well as human beings. As with the traditional *Bildungsheld,* this passage into the land of trials represents "the beginning of the long and really perilous path of initiatory conquests and moments of illumination" (Campbell, 109). The journey leads Trini to the Valley of San Domingo, "bleak and bare," "dreary, interminable grey" hills enclosed by a desert, "a brown dry world" (81). It is in this barren wasteland, reminiscent of what Northrop Frye calls "the natural sterility of a fallen world" (189), the symbolic physical and psychological antithesis to the green valley of her childhood, that Trini undergoes her first trial, her sexual initiation.

In this valley an Indian girl is being held at the local brothel, El Jardín de Venus. The fact that the girl is said to have no name only underscores that women are both invisible and powerless in a patriarchal system .[3] In their refusal to take pity on the girl, however, village women show their own conditioned complicity with patriarchal abuse of women and their alienation from their own status as women. When Trini helps the Indian girl to flee, she is attacked and violently raped. She eventually escapes, but when she tries to report the crime to the authorities, the policeman, "suggestive and lewd" (107), insinuates that being fifteen she probably provoked the sexual violation. This accusation leaves her a "painful chrysalis of helplessness and anger" (107) as it becomes clear that she, a woman, a mestiza, can claim no rights when it comes to socially sanctioned male prerogatives in respect to women. Trini's sexual initiation, rather than being a life-affirming experience, thus becomes a violent introduction into the conditions of womanhood.

Sexual initiation, playing an essential role in human development, represents one of the thematic features of the *Bildungsroman*. This inevitable initiation, however, often carries dramatically different implications for the female adolescent. Trini's sexual initiation is representative of a recurrent theme in female *Bildungsromane*, that is, the sexual violation. Sexual initiation in male *Bildungsromane* is generally portrayed as the adolescent protagonist's initiation into manhood, in other words, the initial proof of male prowess and power and therefore an affirmation of his male identity according to socio-sexual patriarchal ideology; a "hot-blooded taking" of a woman, sexual aggression, is thus portrayed as a sort of "baptism of fire in passion . . . the baptism of life" (Buckley, 208). For the female adolescent protagonist, however, the sexual initiation frequently carries quite different implications: physically weaker than her male counterpart, her initiation is often forced upon her against her will. Whereas a "hot-blooded taking" of a woman supposedly confirms manhood in an adolescent male, for the female adolescent, the object of such aggression, a forced sexual initiation becomes not only a physical violation, but a denigration of her integrity and personal identity as a woman. Her inability to avenge herself further underscores her defenselessness within a system that sanctions the violation of the female self in its physical and psychological integrity. Her sexual initiation is thus not a positive initiation into womanhood, but rather her initiation into the conditions of womanhood within a patriarchal system.

In Mexican and Chicano mythology, however, the metaphor of

rape carries further significance as it associates the Chicana with the archetypal Malinche figure, also known as Doña Marina, who, according to legend, "politically and sexually betrayed indigenous Mexico by becoming Cortes' mistress on the eve of Spanish conquest" (Limón, 59). Through this legend the Malinche has come to represent, according to Octavio Paz, "the *Chingada*, . . . the Mother forcibly opened, violated or deceived" (79). This myth associates cultural/sexual rape with a woman's betrayal of her own people, a legend that has given shape to the Malinche archetype in Mexican/Chicano mythology.[4] Within this cultural framework rape thus carries a double meaning in that it signifies not only a violation of the female self but becomes a symbol of collective rape. As Elizabeth Ordóñez maintains,

> if rape has become a powerful image of woman's
> helplessness and subjugation before the sheer brute force of
> the male, then that universal trauma for all women becomes
> exacerbated in the Chicana experience by those remnants of
> the collective physical and cultural rape which she carries
> buried within her collective unconscious. (328)

The psycho-mythological implications of Trini's sexual initiation are hinted at in the names Héctor and El Jardín de Venus. In Greek mythology Hector is the ideal warrior, characterized as a good son, a loving husband and father, and a trusty friend, and Venus, the goddess of fertility and love. In *Trini*, however, Héctor takes on the opposite characteristics and becomes the embodiment of a misogynous villain, while the Garden of Venus becomes the physical manifestation of sexual exploitation. That the rapist is a Eurocentric mythic hero is an implicit evocation of the cultural violation that the act of rape stands for in Mexican/Chicano mythology.

This use of mythical characters and the reversal of their general mythic identity are indicative of both the mythical nature of female development and the opposite nature of female sexual initiation, and typifies what Annis Pratt calls "the rape-trauma archetype" of female development. The fact that this rape-trauma archetype is "one of the most frequent plot structures in women's fiction" (1981, 5) testifies to the significance of sexual violation in female development. Rather than following "the path of initiatory conquest," which defines the male heroic quest according to Campbell, the female heroic quest may be defined as following a path of initiatory defeats in which sexual subjugation plays a central role and stands as a metaphor for patriarchal violation of female identity that foreshadows a distinct female *Bildungs* course.

The sexual violation has a traumatic effect on Trini, yet it becomes a catalyst in her decision to forge her own destiny. Her dreams of a life reminiscent of that of her childhood having come to naught, dreams that included the Indian Sabochi as her loving mate, she is determined to put her negative experiences behind her, to find "a way out of old disappointments" (133) and shape a life of her own. Her decision to depart for the city provokes an essential confrontation with her father, who wants her to remain within the realm of family and cultural traditions. Although she has always identified with her father's beliefs and way of life, shaped by "Indian ways, Indian rhythms of the blood" (133), it becomes clear to her that a search for an authentic self includes breaking away from his way of life in an attempt to explore her own mestiza identity: "She didn't want to love all that was Indian anymore. She would learn about the city, become the city, learn to prefer her white blood" (133); doubts notwithstanding, she is determined to become a "city girl" and make a life for herself in the city. The journey that started in Bachotigori, the valley of her happy childhood, and led her to San Domingo, the valley of her violent sexual initiation, thus brings her to Chihuahua, the city where new challenges and trials will have a decisive influence on her *Bildungs* process.

In Chihuahua Trini becomes acquainted with women whose sole point of reference seems to be their respective husbands or lovers;

the relationship to a man, or lack of the same, is the principal determinant of their lives. Within this circle of women, getting a *casita* is quite an accomplishment: "It was hard to find a man to set up a house for you, to pay expenses. Sometimes girls secretly admitted that getting a casita offered more advantages than marriage" (137). Their preference for a *casita* rather than marriage may be interpreted as an example of women's "refusal to abide by capitalist and patriarchal needs of ownership" (Gonzales-Berry, 2), yet a *casita* means only a temporary escape from poverty for these women whose importance is measured by their ability to accommodate to the roles of wife, mother, and/or sexual object. In the barrio the visible signs of poor women's economic dependency in exchange for sexual favors are omnipresent: "Casitas were sprinkled in all the poor neighborhoods where they stood out like sore thumbs with their fresh paint, picket fences, gardens, and many of the luxuries the poor could not afford" (141). Life seems to offer only two accessible options to the women of this poverty stricken barrio: either you marry or you become a paid mistress.

These economic and cultural conditions that divide the female population into either wives/mothers or whores are most clearly represented through Trini's roommates, Licha and Celia. The gentle and self-sacrificing Celia has two children and a husband who has contracted cancer from poisonous pesticides in the fields of California; after patiently waiting for his return she nurses him, suffering while she watches him slowly die. Licha, her diametrical opposite, is the embodiment of selfishness: good-looking and calculating, and seeing love as "childish and foolish" (145), she escapes poverty by marrying Don Alejandro, a rich old man whose fortune will provide her with future economic security; emotionally independent, Licha plans her life "like a careful mathematician" (145). This portrayal of Licha as calculating and insensitive is further underscored when later, despite her friendship with Trini, she is presented as the ruthless seductress of Trini's lover. Portillo Trambley here presents a social context where female bonding gives way to female competition for male favors: seeing herself as a male-defined object, Licha can only find a confirmation of her being in the eyes of a man and in her victory over another woman.

It may seem surprising that the author should choose to depict these two women in roles that do not go beyond the traditional stereotypes of Hispanic women. Celia and Licha are prime examples of what Judy Salinas has termed the "good" woman and the "bad" woman (192): Celia, patient and self-denying, can do no wrong and sacrifices herself for others; Licha, insatiate and craving, shuns no means to get what she wants. In the context of Trini's *Bildungs* process, however, these two women represent false role models, the false female prototypes Trini has to overcome in her quest for an authentic self. Both women see themselves as the "other" to a male counterpart, their role as women being realized only through their relationship to a man; although they appear to be diametrically opposite to each other, they only represent two faces of the same coin, as both adhere to male-imposed definitions of womanhood. These female prototypes represent the patriarchal trap of socially sanctioned roles. It therefore becomes crucial for the female protagonist to escape these traditional roles and patriarchal definitions of her female self; only then will she be able to continue her heroic journey toward self-fulfillment.

The test comes in the form of Tonio, a *mujeriego* (womanizer) whom Trini used to know as a child in the valley of Bachotigori. Tonio has his own image of Trini—"you'll always be a *descalza* [literally *barefoot,* or a country girl], in spite of the lipstick and high heels. . . . You are still Tonantzín" (148)—and Trini, now eighteen and searching for a viable self in the city, begins to see herself through his eyes and accepts his definitions of her as her own. In his role as "Prince Charming," Tonio wants "to claim" (149) Trini, and Trini, flattered by his desire for her, acquiesces to his sexual seduction. Although she initially insists that she belongs to herself only, it is not long before she expresses her "joy of belonging" to Antonio (151), of being his desired possession. She automatically takes on the roles of both wife and mistress, existing passively in the shadow of his life, grateful for any attention he chooses to bestow upon her, without being conscious of the true nature of their relationship. It becomes clear, however, when Trini becomes pregnant that he is only interested in having her as a comforting mistress; refusing to give up his independence for a child, he abandons Trini for a new mistress, Licha. Living in an abandoned *casita*, her fate is a repetition of that of the woman who lived there before her, a continuation of a cycle of female dependency. Trini's "joy of belonging" is thus short-lived, making clear the deceptive security these roles have to offer. She is yet another victim of a patriarchal system of female objectification that only fosters rivalry and divides women against each other.

Trini's move to the city, her encounter with false female prototypes, and her subsequent ordeal as she falls into the patriarchal trap of female subordination and dependency, occupy a central phase in her *Bildungs* process. Her determination to come to the city to find herself is obscured by a patriarchal conditioning that is only reinforced by the predominant pattern of behavior among the women she encounters there. Despite her intentions to discover some clues to the meaning of her life, her experiences in the city remove her only further from her goal of personal authenticity. Her urban experience, the corruption and deception of the urban environment, thus contrasts sharply with the harmonious transcendence experienced in the natural setting of her childhood.

Trini's passage from home to the city is reminiscent of a recurrent theme in the traditional male *Bildungsroman*, the city often representing a source of corruption for the initiate. Despite its promise of infinite possibilities and newness, the city, as Buckley points out, "all too often brings disenchantment more alarming and decisive"

(20) than any previous disappointments. In contrast to the male *Bildungsroman,* however, where the city corrupts the character of the protagonist, here it is not the depravity of the city itself that leads Trini astray, but rather its intensification of patriarchal socio-sexual definitions of womanhood. Whereas in male *Bildungsromane* women generally represent only one of the many experiences the city has to offer, here men are the source of female victimization. Trini's experience as Tonio's mistress is essentially an exercise in self-denial, yet, despite the negative implications of this experience, it also becomes an impetus for Trini to continue her quest for authentic selfhood.

The experience of male deception and rejection casts Trini into an emotional turmoil. Deeply wounded in spirit and soul she flees back into nature to seek refuge with her old friend Sabochi. Seeing in him the answer to her confusion and disappointments, she attempts to recapture the idealized love of her childhood. Their encounter becomes the epiphany of mutual love through which she recaptures her sense of oneness with the cosmos. However, with the consummation of their relationship comes also the realization of their essential differences and, contrary to her dreams, that a loving relationship is not enough to fulfill her life: "Their isolation was not life. They only had each other—why wasn't that enough?" (171). This realization makes Trini reflect upon her past in an attempt to find some clue to the meaning of her experiences and her actions. Determined to give "some direction to her life" (160), she begins to shape questions that are crucial for her understanding of the direction her life has taken:

> I reach out—there's nothing there. What's the matter with me? Is it my fault? . . . What drives me on and on and on? A fierceness seemed to rise in her, mute, indecipherable. She folded inward, her mind grappling for answers, for reasons. . . . Tonio and Sabochi had outpaced her, hurtling into lives of their choice without her, without needing her, without wanting her. (166)

Bildung as Entrapment

Taking stock, she recognizes a pattern in her life: that her perception of herself and her own life has depended on a relationship to a man. Acknowledging this dependency is the first crucial step she takes as she begins to imagine a life of her own making: "There's more to life than a man! . . . I have to be much more myself, more than just a woman in love" (171).

Trini's encounter with Sabochi is pivotal in her heroic journey toward self-fulfillment. When Trini in her hopelessness sees no other solution than seeking refuge in Sabochi, she engages in a flight from her own life, a retreat into an idealized romance of her childhood. With the fulfillment of her romantic fantasies comes the realization, however, that her lover cannot fulfill her life and that she has her own life to live. That it is her encounter with Sabochi, with her past, that brings about these realizations adheres closely to what Annis Pratt sees as a basic pattern in women's fiction: Sabochi is the embodiment of the archetypal "green-world lover," the "ideal, nonpatriarchal lover" (1981, 140) who aids at difficult points in the female development. Sabochi helps her understand her dependency on men, and realize that she has to break this dependency in order to create her own life; he constitutes a phase through which she must pass in order to continue her heroic quest for self. Acknowledging a pattern in her life, that her attempts at solutions in the past have always been "to run, to move," she also recognizes that "a journey is never enough," that this is only a part of her development, the journey that will guide her toward what "would someday be the better part" (161). Thus, when spring, the universal symbol of new beginnings, arrives, Trini is pregnant but ready to leave Sabochi, ready to continue her journey, to put into practice her new vision of herself as an independent woman who wants to create a life of her own: "It's all up to me, my life, without Sabochi, without Tonio" (174).

However, upon her return new obstacles challenge her newfound determination to quest for personal independence. Poverty and loneliness weaken her resolution to shape her own life and push her back to Tonio. Hating herself for "falling into the old pattern," she is tempted once more by the words "husband" and "home," by the illusory dream of "security, safety" (175). Trini marries Tonio as if it is a destiny she cannot escape. It is here that the conflict between autonomy and female social conditioning becomes most evident: although she is conscious that marriage is a "mere refuge" for her, and despite the physical abuse she suffers for being pregnant with Sabochi's child, she trusts Tonio's promises more than her own ability to create a life of her own. When Tonio pronounces the words "my wife," a role she passively accepts, he is only asserting the social expectations that have conditioned Trini to view her role as a wife as her only feasible destiny. The image of herself as a wife, her romantic notion of marriage and the supposed security it entails, is powerful and tempting and overshadows any previous determination she might have had to achieve autonomy and self-fulfillment by creating her own life independent of a man.

Trini's situation exemplifies the severe obstacles economic deprivation places on women's independence: she struggles to understand and overcome her dependency on men and the psychological effects of female conditioning, yet as a single mother with a second child on the way she is also facing the harsh reality of destitution, a reality she cannot escape. Her opting for the prospect of future security with Tonio illustrates how "women's marginality leads to economic and social dependency on the male" (Herrera-Sobek, 1988, 175). However, it also shows how Trini, given her social situation, is more vulnerable to the romantic notions of marriage and its promises of "security" and "safety" and thus more likely to fall into the trap of dependency on the male. Trini's previous experiences with Tonio notwithstanding, she takes refuge once more in his promises, yet once more she is confronted with the deceptive nature of such promises: shortly after she joins him in Juárez, he leaves her "to make

Bildung as Entrapment

American money" (181) across the border. Left again to fend for herself, Trini is forced to recognize that she will have to rely on her own resources, that she will find security only in her own self-reliance. If she feels as if she has "journeyed for centuries, her destiny still unshaped," a mere "blur in the future," she also realizes that it is mainly because she has expected a man to shape that destiny. This recognition of her own situation together with a basic need for survival gives her a new determination to continue, "to journey again, to search, to find, to plan" (182).

Necessity forces her to cross the border to work illegally as a domestic in El Paso. Eventually she has to return to Mexico where, destitute and helpless, she ends up in El Terreno de Brujas among retired prostitutes, among "the debris of the world . . . decaying, forgotten" (189). It is significant that it is through this symbolic descent into a "living burial ground" (190) that she is brought into an existential confrontation with herself that reawakens the old dream of land and spiritual wholeness. With a renewed awareness of the supernatural world she had known throughout her childhood, she begins to rely more and more on her own intuition for survival. Among the social outcasts of this "burial ground" she encounters an old prostitute, popularly thought to be a witch, and a dwarf who appears to be a reincarnation of the dwarf Trini used to play with as a child. These two characters become her guides and confirm her notion that, despite all the difficulties and setbacks, there is a design, an ultimate meaning to her trials and her long journey north.

Trini's old dream of land is given further impetus when she hears about the possibility of citizenship "in the land of plenty" (206) if her child is born on the other side of the border. Guided by dreams and following the "intuitive pull" of destiny, her "plan with a dream" (207), Trini succeeds in crossing the border to give birth to a son in El Paso. Utterly destitute, but guided by what she perceives to be cosmic signs, she finds her way to Valverde, the Green Valley, where a dying dwarf, Salvador—whose name translates as "savior," "redeemer"—gives her a piece of land in exchange for her performing his funeral in accordance with indigenous religious rites. Salvador appears to be yet another reincarnation of the dwarf of her childhood, who, through his various appearances, has guided her toward what seems to be the completion of her quest, her final settlement in Valverde. The burning of his dead body thus becomes a ceremony for her arrival in the green valley that holds the promises of self-fulfillment, a ceremony that leaves "a clean, fragrant hope, the trust in a new beginning" (233).

Trini's arrival in Valverde should, according to the paradigm of the traditional quest story, signal the completion of her spiritual and social quest for wholeness. That her journey leads her to a place called Valverde underscores once more the overall psycho-mythological design of this female quest story. Trini's quest—the initial separation, the initiation, the tests she undergoes along the way, and the guides who eventually lead her to the green valley—corresponds in its general design to the basic outlines of Campbell's monomyth, yet the expected self-fulfillment and restoration of lost harmony upon her arrival in Valverde does not materialize. If, according to traditional plot expectations, Trini's arrival in the Green Valley should indicate the happy denouement of her quest, then this female quest story goes beyond the ending, so to speak.

Trini also expects Valverde to be the place where "the better part" of her life will materialize, where she will be able to recapture lost harmony and create her own life: "The journey was over, the land had been found, the family had been gathered. The dream had come true" (235). This fulfillment of her dream for land and a family of her own, however, does not fulfill her quest for self. When we meet her again, nine years later, she has become "la madre abnegada," the hard-working, self-sacrificing wife and mother who works herself "numb to keep her sanity" (236). Tonio, mostly absent, rejects her for other women. Yet, trapped in her dependency on him, she accepts his status as the patriarch of the family who is entitled to do as he pleases. Her submission to him and her conformity to traditional patriarchal expectations lead her to an enslaving role as wife and mother, but only through a denial of her own selfhood. Her precarious situation as a woman and as a *Mexicana*, a stranger in a foreign culture, makes her alienation and loneliness doubly oppressive: estranged from her husband and her five children who are becoming more and more Americanized, her daily life is a struggle "to accept an insurmountable existence that hung, split, folding into loneliness" (235) that is "about to drown her" (244).

It is this sense of disillusionment and suffocation that prompts Trini to examine the confining pattern of her present life with the awareness her experiences have given her. In an act reminiscent of her adolescent search for a viable self, she now, at thirty, returns to the mirror only to refuse to accept her own self-image: "There's more to me" (236), just as there "must be more" (239) than the deceptive pattern of her own life. Her old dream of marriage and family having turned into a suffocating trap, she channels her protest into fantasy and begins to create a new dream to sustain herself. Trini's consciousness is thus divided into an apparent acceptance of patriarchal social structures and a wish to escape the alienation and confinement those structures have imposed upon her life. She wants to escape this alienation, but finding herself at an impasse in her social world, she turns to nature for spiritual wholeness. She takes the first step toward such wholeness when one night she refuses to be a victim and walks out, "her senses awakened to the moon" (244) and to the forces of nature. In this awakening she envisions a return to nature as the only feasible path toward authenticity and selfhood.

This mystical identification with nature has its origins in her childhood when she had identified with the earth and its fertility goddess Tonantzín. Part of her education leads her to forsake indigenous beliefs for Catholicism, to prefer the Catholic Virgin to Tonantzín, yet throughout her quest she remains sensitive to the presence of an indigenous spiritual world. The religious conflict between traditional Catholicism and indigenous beliefs corresponds closely to Trini's cultural conflict as a mestiza: initially torn between the Indian and the white part of herself, she is slowly removed from her indigenous past and learns to see herself as "part of the white man's world" (171). This same *Bildungs* process has led her to accept patriarchal definitions of womanhood, to accept prescribed self-sacrificing and nurturing roles, but at the cost of her own self. It is when Trini awakens to this stultifying and self-effacing existence, an alienation intensified by her additional cultural alienation in the United States, that she reclaims her connection to Tonantzín. This identification with a gyno-centered spiritual sphere allows her to envision a renewed unity with nature as an escape from the confines of patriarchal space. Trini's awakening to the reality of her life is an awakening to limitations. At the denouement of *Trini* her spiritual relationship to nature prevails as the ultimate reality in the life of our female *Bildungsheld.*

In its structural outline *Trini* adheres to the linear paradigm of the traditional male *Bildungsroman* by tracing a personal development from childhood to maturity. Much like the traditional male *Bildungsheld* Trini is orphaned, leaves the ideal setting of her childhood, and sets out on a perilous quest for identity. Unlike her male counterpart, however, Trini has to undergo trials that do not further her *Bildungs* process, but rather remove her further and further away from authenticity and selfhood. Throughout the novel there is a recurrent oppositional tension between, on the one hand, Trini's search for a viable self, and on the other hand, social demands of submission to the confines of a male culture. Trini's quest for identity is thus disrupted at every stage by what Pratt calls the "hidden agenda of gender norms" (1981, 16) of dependency and submission. Trini encounters a world defined by patriarchal prerogatives inimical to female independence, a fundamental discrepancy between social demands and her own search for selfhood, or in Rosowski's terms, a "disparity between her needs as a human being and the role expected of her as a woman" (328). Driven by relentless social pressures into seeing herself defined by love and marriage, Trini is caught in a world of "enclosure and atrophy" (Pratt, 1981, 16). When she awakens to this "drowning" of herself, only a withdrawal into nature seems to offer the possibility of a personal transformation and self-fulfillment.

The traditional *Bildungsroman* is a genre in which "social realism is apt to become mixed with elements of romance" (Pratt, 1981, 13). This mixture of social realism and romance is reflected in the prototypical *Bildungsroman* plot: the successful completion of the *Bildungs* quest is an affirmation of the hero's manhood and autonomy and includes romantic interludes that often lead to marriage and general accommodations to social values. This is also the case when we turn to the basic patterns of Northrop Frye's "Mythos of Romance," the successful quest myth: the hero undergoes a perilous journey—agon, pathos, anagnorisis—then emerges empowered from his quest, the reward of which "usually is or includes a bride" (N. Frye, 193) with whom he supposedly lives happily ever after. These romantic plot conventions—that is, the active male quester, the passive female, and the concluding marriage—are also governing features of most fairy tales and romantic stories, which both reflect and reinforce cultural paradigms of gender roles and behaviors. The leading assumption behind these socio-cultural expectations reflected in literary plot conventions is that marriage is an additional aspect of the male quest, whereas to the female hero marriage is presented as "not simply one ideal, but the only estate toward which women should aspire" (Rowe,

239). Social accommodations through marriage, however, have additional dramatic consequences for the female hero than for her male counterpart:

> *Because* the heroine adopts conventional female virtues, that is, patience, sacrifice, and dependency, and *because* she submits to patriarchal needs, she consequently receives both the prince and guarantee of social and financial security through marriage. (Rowe, 246)

Since this so-called "happy ending" in marriage can only be obtained through female submission to the patriarchal status quo, the traditional romantic plot structure stands in direct opposition to the female quest for identity and selfhood.

In both *Victuum* and *Trini* the generic mixture of social realism and romance is reflected in the romantic plot conventions that direct the development of the female protagonists toward marriage and family. At the end of a traditional female *Bildung,* womanhood is defined not through selfhood and autonomy, but by a gradual succumbing to social norms and prescriptions of female behavior. The *Bildungs* process in both *Victuum* and *Trini* is governed by this, it seems, inevitable path toward marriage, which, at the same time, leads the protagonists away from an autonomous female identity. Throughout her childhood and adolescence Valentina in *Victuum* is prepared for her future role as wife and mother, a role she seemingly accepts with the same inevitability as she later accepts the authority of her husband to control her life. Trini undergoes a similar preparation throughout her adolescence, but unlike Valentina, Trini comes to question her own relationship to men and her position as a woman in a male-dominated world; she is, nevertheless, relentlessly driven toward becoming a mother and a submissive wife. Both protagonists go through a *Bildungs* process that unequivocally leads toward an apparent predestined future of marriage and maternity.

Victuum and *Trini* are woman-centered novels of the female quest for selfhood, yet the process of growing up female portrayed in these two novels does not lead to the expected affirmation of self, but rather to alienation of self. This narrative plot of female development, positioned within a male-defined tradition, thus reflects both the "ideological underpinnings" (J. Frye, 1) of the traditional *Bildungs* story and the larger socio-cultural context that circumscribes an authentic female *Bildung*. Bound by socio-cultural assumptions and economic constraints, the protagonists here are doomed to follow a prescribed path of female development, as they are not invested with a consciousness that would enable them to resist or take an oppositional stance against social norms and definitions of female behavior. Thus growing up female leads to socio-cultural entrapment, exemplifying Joanne Frye's contention that "the power of a male-dominated sexual ideology entraps women characters and women novelists within outworn plots and outworn definitions; women in novels—and even in life—seem doomed to live within those old stories" (5). These two Chicana *Bildungsromane* variously illustrate that as long as the *Bildungs* process is not accompanied by an evolving consciousness about women's position in a manmade world it is most likely to lead to socio-cultural entrapment.

Not withstanding their socio-cultural entrapment, both *Victuum* and *Trini* circumvent in the end the paradigms of a male-defined genre and lead the protagonists beyond prescribed norms of womanhood: through a mid-life awakening of self, Valentina and Trini are given an alternative vision of selfhood, a vision of escape that signals a rejection of existing patterns and, in terms of the female quest story, a rejection of "outworn plots and outworn definitions." Valentina seeks awareness and self-fulfillment in the psychic sphere, a process of self-awakening that Bonnie Hoover Braendlin recognizes as central to women's quest for wholeness:

> When a fictional woman reaches an impasse in her quest for
> freedom and self-determination, when her linear journey in
> the world of experience leads to an enslaving, fragmenting

role as wife and mother, there still remains open to her the alternative of an inward journey to the depths of the psyche. (20)

Trini reaches this same impasse in her social existence, but perceives a return to nature as the only feasible alternative to socio-cultural alienation and the "drowning" of her own self. Although each *Bildungs* process leads to socio-cultural entrapment, both novels subvert in the end the traditional *Bildungsroman* plot pattern by showing Chicana lives as an ongoing process whose reach carries beyond passive entrapment and the traditional ending in marriage and cultural accommodation.

These two novels present both an implicit and explicit critique of the patriarchal system. More rooted in the mundane, *Trini* shows a process of entrapment that is assured by two tiers of oppression—the economic and the psychological dependency on the oppressor—and suggests thereby that an authentic female *Bildungsroman* will not materialize until these twin yokes of oppression are thrown off. *Victuum*, in turn, never overtly articulates a critique of such socio-cultural entrapment, but the reader can interpret Valentina's flight into the interior psychic world as a resistance to entrapment and a quest beyond social roles for an authentic interior self. Neither woman is in the end fully realized, but both novels suggest that in order to realize the self it is necessary for women to get in touch with the original intuition of being. For Valentina this original intuition of being is located in the psychic realm, whereas Trini finds it in her connection to nature.

Victuum and *Trini* are women-centered novels where women are, to use Bell Hooks's phrase, moved from the margin to the center and given the power of speech central to female self-definition, yet each individual voice is very much determined by the socio-cultural expectations to which the protagonists succumb in the process of their development. In the end Valentina and Trini are marginalized solitary figures who withdraw into an extra-social existence. Their with-drawal exemplifies Annis Pratt's contention that the female *Bildungsheld*

> does not *choose* a life to one side of society after conscious deliberation on the subject; rather, she is ontologically or radically alienated by gender-role norms from *the very outset*. Thus, although the authors attempt to accommodate their hero's *Bildung*, or development, to the general pattern of the genre, the disjunctions . . . inevitably make the woman's initiation less a self-determined progression *towards* maturity than a regression *from* full participation in adult life. (1981, 36)

Such regression characterizes the denouement of both *Victuum* and *Trini* and situates these two Chicana *Bildungshelde* in a long line of female protagonists who have been caught in a conflict between "that outward existence which conforms, and the inward life which questions" (Chopin, *The Awakening*, 14). This fundamental conflict between patriarchal demands and female authenticity that impels Valentina and Trini to seek sustenance and selfhood in an extra-social sphere demonstrates the disjunction between the generic intent of the traditional *Bildungsroman* and the socio-cultural realities that inform the female developmental process.

Portraying Chicana self-development from approximately 1920 to 1960, these two Chicana *Bildungsromane* situate their female protagonists in circumstances that correspond to different aspects of the Chicano historical background: one is kept firmly within the extended family of an old Hispanic community in California; the other follows the migratory path north through Mexico and into the United States. Given the particular time and place of their setting, both novels show a Chicana *Bildungs* process that is bound by powerful economic and socio-cultural constraints. Lacking visions of alternative destinies for women, the protagonists succumb to cultural expectations in respect to their own gender formation and socio-cultural role and become submissive, self-sacrificing, and dependent. Although both protagonists go through a mid-life awakening that may lead to personal liberation, their initial entrapment differs decisively from the developmental process of other Chicana *Bildungshelde* whose quest for a self-defined identity is formed through a conscious opposition to patriarchal confinement of the female self.

.

PART II
BILDUNG AS A SUBVERSIVE ACT

Things are starting to be written, things that will constitute a feminine Imaginary, the site, that is, of identification of an ego no longer given over to an image defined by the masculine . . . but rather inventing forms for women on the march, or as I prefer to fantasize, "in flight," so that instead of lying down, women will go forward by leaps in search of themselves.

—Hélène Cixous

With the publication of *The House on Mango Street* (1985) by Sandra Cisneros and *The Last of the Menu Girls* (1986) by Denise Chávez, the Chicana *Bildungsroman* turns away from patterning the female quest story on the traditional male-defined generic paradigm of individual accommodation to socio-cultural values and gender role expectations to portray the *Bildung* of a Chicana as a process of self-discovery that is a conscious quest for authentic female selfhood. If we, in the previous two novels of this study, encountered only a muted resistance to a *Bildungs* process that confined the protagonists to socio-cultural norms of womanhood, the protagonists in *The House on Mango Street* and *The Last of the Menu Girls* openly resist such confinement by daring to voice what previously had remained unspoken in respect to the process of growing up as a Chicana.

For a female *Bildungsroman* to portray an authentic female *Bildungs* process that leads to self-discovery and self-definition, the protagonist must necessarily subvert patriarchal traditions and definitions of the female self, "the seemingly inescapable patterns, images, plots, and forms in which female 'heroines' are inevitably caught" (Heller, 26). She must subvert the traditional female quest story that confines the female hero to "a thwarted or impossible journey, a rude awakening to limits, and a reconciliation to society's expectations of female passivity and immobility" (Heller, 14). Such subversion of the traditional female *Bildungs* story is made possible when the protagonist becomes the narrator of her own text. When the female "I" is the central consciousness of a *Bildungsroman,* the rendering of the female *Bildungs* process is based on a female experiential perspective: the oppositional nature of the interaction between the female self and socio-cultural values and gender role expectations is not presented by an external and distanced omniscient narrator, but based on and interpreted by the complex subjectivity of the female *Bildungsheld.* By assuming the role of the narrator/protagonist, the female "I" becomes the conscious subject of her own *Bildungs* story who, through the act of narrating, actively participates in the process of her own self-formation. When the female "I" takes on narrative authority, she gains authority over her own life and her own story, an act which in and of itself subverts patriarchal confinement of the female self.

In both *The House on Mango Street* and *The Last of the Menu Girls* the Chicana protagonist becomes the narrator of her own *Bildungs* experiences. In each of these two *Bildungsromane* the Chicana narrator/protagonist is a conscious being who, through the act of questioning and interpreting her socio-cultural context, gains a new understanding of herself and her position in the world as a Chicana. As the central consciousness of the text, the narrator/protagonist is the agent of her own story who takes on narrative authority in respect to what aspects of her life and her experiences as a Chicana are meaningful to her own *Bildungs* process. Crucial to this process of discovery of self within a socio-cultural context is the narrator's conscious exploration of the contradictions between the internal perception of self and the external definitions of womanhood, contradictions which the Chicana narrator/protagonist interprets through her own experiential perspective. In both *The House on Mango Street* and *The Last of the Menu Girls,* the protagonist is the narrative authority who voices the socio-cultural contradictions and affirmations that form part of her life as a Chicana, and as such she becomes an active agent in the formation of her own cultural and gender identity.

In these two Chicana *Bildungsromane* the narrator/protagonist's openly subjective act of shaping and narrating her own *Bildungs* story in rejection of external definitions is accompanied by narrative strategies that stand in opposition to the traditional linear, chronological convention of the genre. Each novel consists of a collection of short narratives told by the narrating "I" that focuses on particular essential experiences or episodes in the narrator/protagonist's life. In adopting this narrative strategy, the author underscores the fragmented, nonlinear nature of the female *Bildungs* process. This disruption of male-defined generic paradigms substantiates Judith Kegan Gardiner's argument that "women writers re-create female experiences in different forms," a development that seems to be "a direct result of their different developmental experience" (1981, 355). In their portrayal of the Chicana *Bildungs* process, *The House on Mango Street* and *The Last of the Menu Girls* thus subvert both in content and form "the confining expectations of both narrative and life" (J. Frye, 83), that is, the traditional gender as well as genre limitations of the female quest story.

It is not enough, however, for the female *Bildungs* process to refute old patterns and images or to break "the rules to somebody else's game" (Ordóñez, 20): breaking away from the old, the female *Bildungsheld* must also be able to imagine new future possibilities for herself. In his study of the (male) *Bildungsroman,* Buckley considers a "gradual imaginative enlightenment" (281) essential to the hero's initiation. Such "imaginative enlightenment" is particularly pertinent when it comes to the female quest for self-definition. Lacking role models, it is through an act of the imagination that the female protagonist must envision her own liberation, her own future of independence and self-realization; in other words, the female *Bildungsheld* must imagine herself into being. Adrienne Rich speaks to this need for affirmative visions of the future as a sine qua non in women's resistance to entrapment when she argues that "if the imagination is to transcend and transform experience it has to question, to challenge, to conceive of alternatives" (43). Resisting old roles while imagining new ones is thus essential to an autonomous female self-definition.

It is perhaps not surprising then that the Chicana narrators/protagonists in *The House on Mango Street* and *The Last of the Menu Girls* are aspiring writers who, through creative imagination, project their future selves beyond the boundaries of the status quo of their socio-cultural contexts. Each is the budding artist who, through her own creative perspective, is able to turn her *Bildung* into a process of liberating self-creation. Through the act of narrating/writing the text, the Chicana protagonist of each of these novels, speaking in her own voice of her own experiences, claims her subjective difference, her identity as a unique, self-defined person, and her cultural identity as a Chicana; the text thus becomes the medium for "the definition of the individual subjectivity" as well as "the articulation of collective experience and identity" (Yarbro-Bejarano, 144). This interplay between self-development and the creative imagination of the young artist turns each of these two novels into a *Künstlerroman*, that is, the portrayal of the development of an individual who becomes—or is on the threshold of becoming—an artist of some kind. The Chicana "I," the narrator/protagonist/artist, is "her own midwife, creating herself anew" (Rich, 35), forging in the process a new relationship between self and community.

Bildung as a Subversive Act

3

THE HOUSE ON MANGO STREET
A Space of Her Own

By writing I put order in the world, give it a handle so I can grasp it. I write to record what others erase when I speak, to rewrite the stories others have miswritten about me, about you. To discover myself, to preserve myself, to make myself, to achieve self-autonomy.

—GLORIA ANZALDÚA

The House on Mango Street (1985) by Sandra Cisneros is probably the best-known Chicana novel to date. The winner of the American Book Award in 1985, it has received more critical attention than any other Chicana novel. Set in a contemporary Latino neighborhood of a big American city, *The House on Mango Street* is composed of forty-four interrelated stories narrated by Esperanza, the female "I" and central consciousness of the novel.[1] In each story Esperanza narrates her own perception of her socio-cultural context, that is, the barrio, its people, its conditions of life, and how she is inextricably connected to that context, an engagement with her immediate surroundings that brings about a gradual coming into consciousness about her own identity as a woman and as a Chicana. Sandra Cisneros gives voice to the ordinary experiences of a young Chicana by letting Esperanza tell her own coming-of-age story, thus articulating the subjective experiences of the female "I" who resists entrapment within socio-cultural norms and expectations. The narrating "I" stands in a dialectic relationship to her socio-cultural context, and it is through the very act of constructing and telling her own story that Esperanza resolves the contradictions that inform her life. Her *Bildungs* process is thus closely linked to her development as an artist in the process of discovering, synthesizing, and narrating her experiences within the community of Mango Street, a development that turns *The House on Mango Street* into what we may call "a portrait of the artist as a young woman," that is, a *Künstlerroman*. It is through the process of telling her stories that Esperanza discovers the power of her own creativity, that "language is a way of becoming" (Seator, 32), a way of imagining herself beyond the confinements of the status quo, a way of imagining a different ending to her own *Bildungs* story. Collectively these stories reveal a female *Bildungs* process that moves from rejection of prescribed roles to the recognition of creativity as a path toward a self-defined identity.

As the title indicates, both "the house" and "Mango Street" are central symbols throughout the novel. Mango Street and the house Esperanza lives in constitute her world, the world she has to come to grips with as she grows up. It is her response to this particular environment, the interplay between psychological and social forces, that determines the direction of her *Bildungs* process. It is through her dialectical relationship to the house—in other words, the private sphere, the family, the collective memory—as well as to Mango Street—that is, the social sphere, the larger Hispanic community—that the narrating "I" comes to an understanding of her own individual self. Esperanza's world on Mango Street is a world unto its own, an Hispanic barrio of a large American city, yet unspecified in respect to its exact geographical and historical setting, a symbolic "microcosm for the larger world" (Gonzales-Berry and Rebolledo, 114) that lends a universal quality to this Chicana *Bildungsroman*.

It is significant that the initial word in this Chicana quest novel is "We": "We didn't always live on Mango Street" (7). Esperanza recalls her family history of moving from one dilapidated house to another until they finally move into their own house on Mango Street, yet the house is not what the family had hoped for: "The house on Mango Street is ours. . . . But even so, it's not the house we'd thought we'd get" (7). Esperanza's sense of self is here firmly lodged within the collective identity of her family. It is, however, in this initial story, homonymous with the novel itself, that the narrating "I" becomes aware of her own subjective perceptions as she begins to differentiate between family dreams and social realities and becomes conscious of her parents' inability to fulfill their promises of the perfect house. "They always told us that one day we would move into a house, a real house" (7). The "real house" Esperanza expected would be "like the houses on TV":

> Our house would be white with trees around it, a great big yard and grass growing without a fence. This was the house Papa talked about when he held a lottery ticket and this was the house Mama dreamed up in the stories she told us before we went to bed.
> But the house on Mango Street is not the way she told it at all. (8)

The house is just the opposite of what she had been told would be their house one day, a fact that stands in direct opposition to the words of her parents. This contrast between expectation and reality awakens her awareness of herself as a social being and provokes her own interpretations of the significance the house holds in her life.

Esperanza sees the house on Mango Street as a symbol of poverty that she associates with the humiliation she has felt in the past, living in similar places:

> Where do you live? she said.
> There, I said, pointing up to the third floor.
> You live *there*?
> *There*. I had to look to where she pointed—the third, the paint peeling, wooden bars Papa had nailed on the windows so we wouldn't fall out.

You live *there*? The way she said it made me feel like nothing. *There.* I lived *there*. I nodded. (8–9)

In another situation a teacher prejudicially assumes that Esperanza, because she is Chicana, lives in a building that "even the raggedy men are ashamed to go into" (43), thus automatically identifying her with the poverty and degradation the house represents. Made to feel ashamed of living in houses other people show obvious contempt for, thus ashamed of "her entire social and subject position" (Saldívar, 1990, 182), Esperanza sees the house as a symbol of the shame that threatens her own self-perception. To Esperanza the house on Mango Street is an emblem of the oppressive socio-economic situation that circumscribes her life and is the source of her feelings of alienation. It is this alienation that becomes a catalyst for her desire to distance herself from this "sad red house" (101) she does not want to belong to.

This psychological rejection of the house on Mango Street is further underscored by her own description of the house as narrow and confining, where even the windows appear to be "holding their breath" (8), a description that shows an almost claustrophobic reaction to her parents' house. According to Cirlot, breathing is a process whereby one assimilates spiritual power. Esperanza's perception of the house as not breathing is indicative of the spiritual suffocation the house represents. This depiction of the house is, as Julián Olivares points out, "a metonymical description and presentation of the self" (162), a self that feels constrained as well as ashamed when identified with a house that represents only confinement and therefore knows that she needs another house, one that would liberate her from the oppression of her present situation:

I knew then I had to have a house. A real house. One I could point to. But this isn't it. The house on Mango Street isn't it. For the time being, Mama said. Temporary, said Papa. But I know how these things go. (9)

Bildung as a Subversive Act

The last phrase, "But I know . . . ," indicates the emerging consciousness of the protagonist, that her passage from childhood innocence to knowledge has begun, a development that marks the beginning of her *Bildungs* process. Through her own interpretative agency she now knows that she cannot rely on what her parents tell her and that they will not be able to provide her with the house that she needs. Although at this point she imagines a "real house" to be something like the Dick and Jane reader's version of an American home, the importance of the house lies not so much in its physical features as in its symbolic value in a socio-cultural context. Her desire for a house is, as Ellen McCracken points out, "not a sign of individualistic acquisitiveness" (64); she wants a house she can "point to," that is, one she can point to as hers without feeling "like nothing" (9), one that does not destroy her sense of self, clearly connecting the house with her own self-perception. By rejecting the house of her parents she rejects a structure that threatens her sense of self and takes the first step toward claiming her right to self-definition.

In this initial story, "The House on Mango Street," the image of the house serves a twofold symbolic function: it is a symbol of the socio-economic condition in which Esperanza finds herself and its alienating effect on her, and more importantly in the context of the novel, as a symbol of human consciousness. Her search for a new house, that is, her search for a viable self, becomes a leitmotif throughout the novel. It is significant that in the course of the story the initial "we," Esperanza's sense of herself being part of the collective identity of her family, gives way to the subjective "I" who begins to analyze her neighborhood on Mango Street.

Like the house, Mango Street is the physical and psychological marker of an oppressive socio-economic situation that makes Esperanza conscious of her own status in a socio-economic hierarchy: "The neighborhood is getting bad," she says, and this is why people have to move "a little farther away every time people like us keep moving in" (15). Much as with the house, a negative analogy is established between Esperanza and her barrio; she lives there and therefore the neighborhood is "getting bad," the narrating "I" again being defined by her external, socio-economic circumstances:

> Those who don't know any better come into our neighborhood scared. They think we're dangerous. They think we will attack them with shiny knives. They are stupid people who are lost and got here by mistake. (29)

The implications of being defined by a poor, deteriorating neighborhood and prejudicial stereotypes make Esperanza conscious of the particular socio-economic conditions that circumscribe her life and trap her in a marginalized world of "too much sadness and not enough sky" (33).

Despite the cumulative threat the house and Mango Street present to her sense of self, however, she begins to imagine herself beyond Mango Street, determined to "make the best of it" (33). Estranged by the social implications of living in this environment, Esperanza disavows her relationship to Mango Street—"I don't ever want to come from here" (99)—identifying herself with the only piece of nature present in the barrio, four trees "who do not belong here but are here":

> Their strength is secret. . . . When I am a tiny thing against so many bricks, then it is I look at trees. When there is nothing left to look at on this street. Four who grew despite concrete. Four who reach and do not forget to reach. (71)

This identification with a small piece of nature in this urban environment exemplifies the primacy of nature in female development, when the adolescent feels "a sense of oneness with cosmos" (Pratt, 1981, 17) as an alternative to her alienation from an oppressive environment. In her longing to escape her present circumstances, Esperanza sees the trees as role models for her own liberation: they grow "despite concrete," thus symbolizing Esperanza's own struggle to grow in a hostile environment, her desire to reach beyond the concrete, beyond class and race boundaries, for self-definition.

Esperanza's process of individuation is thus initiated by her resolution to escape the confinements of her socio-economic condition
represented by the house and by Mango Street, and she does this by
seeking refuge in her own imagination:

> I like to tell stories. I tell them inside my head. . . . I make a
> story for my life, for each step my brown shoe takes. I say,
> "And so she trudged up the wooden stairs, her sad brown
> shoes taking her to the house she never liked." I like to tell
> stories. I am going to tell you a story about a girl who didn't
> want to belong. (101)

It is through the process of making "a story for my life," that is, the
imaginative re-creation of her own experiences and interactions with
her environment, that the narrating "I" begins her search for meaning and a new way of being in the world. Through the act of partici-
pating, interpreting, and narrating her life, she gradually comes to
an understanding of herself and her relationship to the community
on Mango Street.

Esperanza makes a clear link between language and identity when
she turns to the act of narrating her experiences on Mango Street
from her own experiential perspective as a strategy to escape social
oppression and the threat this oppression presents to her own budding sense of self. Naming her own experiences is a way of defining
and validating these experiences as well as her own perspectives. It
is, at the same time, an affirmation of her own being that is grounded
in language, in a new naming of self and her socio-cultural reality.

In this process of constructing herself as a subject through language, she begins to analyze the significance of her name, Esperanza,
as a marker of her own identity. Her attempt to decode the meaning
of her name becomes an attempt to come to terms with her bicultural identity:

> In English my name means hope. In Spanish it means . . .
> sadness, it means waiting. . . . It is the Mexican records my

father plays on Sunday mornings when he is shaving, songs like sobbing. . . . At school they say my name funny as if the syllables were made out of tin and hurt the roof of your mouth. But in Spanish my name is made out of a softer something like silver. (12, 13)

To Esperanza her name embodies contradictory meanings—hope or sadness and waiting—much as the very pronunciation of her name changes with language and cultural context. Her name is thus a sign of a complex bicultural context that requires her to negotiate among opposing cultural meanings to come to terms with her own self.

This multiplicity of meanings that intersect in her name is further underscored by the female legacy the name Esperanza carries in the family. Named after her Mexican great-grandmother, Esperanza is linked through her name to her cultural past and to her identity as a woman within a particular socio-cultural context. The grandmother, a recurring character in Chicana literature, often figures as the embodiment of Chicano cultural heritage: "For the most part *abuelitas* form a complex of female figures who are nurturing, comforting, and stable. They are linked symbolically and spatially to the house and home, and are often associated with an idealized cultural space" (Rebolledo, 1987, 150). In the story Esperanza has inherited about her great-grandmother, however, her *bisabuelita* does not inhabit such an idealized cultural space:

My great-grandmother. I would've liked to have known her, a wild horse of a woman, so wild she wouldn't marry until my great-grandfather threw a sack over her head and carried her off. Just like that, as if she were a fancy chandelier. That's the way he did it. And the story goes she never forgave him. She looked out the window all her life, the way so many women sit their sadness on an elbow. (12)

This story of her namesake, of a strong and rebellious woman who nevertheless had to succumb to patriarchal coercion and control, makes Esperanza conscious of the position women in general hold within her own cultural framework, that the fact that "Mexicans don't like their women strong" (12) kept her great-grandmother from being "all the things she wanted to be" (12). Esperanza links her great-grandmother's fate, her confinement, her sadness and lost hope, with her own name, that is, her self, making her name tantamount to her culture's definitions of gender roles, definitions she can only reject: "Esperanza. I have inherited her name, but I don't want to inherit her place by the window" (12). She thus makes a clear distinction between the wild great-grandmother she would have liked to have known, her cultural foremother, and the socio-cultural system that subdued her. By accepting her name, but refusing to accept a heritage of female confinement, Esperanza carries on a metonymic legacy of rebellion against patriarchal definitions of female selfhood.

In the process of analyzing the significance of the conflicting cultural connotations that intersect in her name—hope, sadness, rebellion, confinement—Esperanza becomes conscious of a complex, and, to her, confusing cultural framework that calls forth some ambivalence in respect to her own cultural heritage. This ambivalence is suggestive of a complicated relationship between ethnic heritage and female quest for a self-defined identity. If one's name is, as Mary Dearborn argues, "inextricable from identity" (93), then Esperanza's name carries some cultural implications that threaten her identity as a woman. She does not, as Renato Rosaldo points out, "stand in one place, looking straight ahead, and shout, 'Yo soy Esperanza'" (163), as that would mean, among other things, embracing patriarchal values and patriarchal definitions of herself. Rather, her ruminations on the cultural implications of her name lead her to wish for a new naming of herself: "I would like to baptize myself under a new name, a name more like the real me, the one nobody sees. . . . Something like Zeze the X will do" (13). Her choice of name, Zeze the X, indicates that what she wants is a name that carries no contradicting cultural connotations; it is, culturally speaking, a "hollow" name she would have to invest with meaning and identity, and unlike her name "Esperanza," it is not "culturally embedded in a dominating, male-centered ideology" (Olivares, 163). Much as she wants a new house, one she can point to, so she wants to give herself a new name that is more attuned to herself, "the one nobody sees." This desire is indicative of her refusal to be externally defined either by her house, by her socio-economic circumstances, or by her name, that is, by traditional patriarchal values, in her quest for a self-defined identity.

In her exploration of the "real" Esperanza, the emerging female self "nobody sees" (13), the narrating "I" becomes increasingly aware of her own emerging sexuality. Her biological transformation marks a crucial point in Esperanza's self-development, as it is then that she begins to note not only her own sexual difference but also its implications for her as a woman.

The first notions of the changes her body is undergoing fill her with expectancy: "Everything is holding its breath inside me. Everything is waiting to explode like Christmas. I want to be all new and shiny" (71); she feels like "a new Buick with the keys in the ignition. Ready to take you where?" (47). This last question is crucial, indicating Esperanza's own awareness of the importance of sexuality in her own development and to her future self, as it is exactly through the control of female sexuality that women are socialized into accepting culturally prescribed roles of wives and mothers. The threat sexuality presents to the female self appears within the context of play when Esperanza and her friends, dressed in "magic high heels," are confronted with men who "can't take their eyes" off them and a "bum man" who says, "come closer. I can't see very well. Come closer. Please. . . . If I give you a dollar will you kiss me?" (39). This scene, with the shoes as symbols of female sexuality and the man's attempt to lure her closer, is a Chicana version of "Little Red Riding Hood," the fairy tale about "the curbing and regulation of sexual drives . . . that has always been used as a warning to children, particularly girls, a symbol and embodiment of what might happen if they are disobedient and careless. She epitomizes the good girl gone wrong" (Zipes, 1). Esperanza's confrontation with the "bum man" becomes an implicit demonstration of the danger sexuality, in a patriarchal context, presents to her own sense of self.

Through her interactions with Sally, Esperanza becomes increasingly aware that her friend already adheres to prescribed feminine behavior and has "her own game" (89), which, as it turns out, is not "her own game" but a male game into which she enters:

> One of the boys invented the rules. One of Tito's friends said you can't get the keys back unless you kiss us and Sally pretended to be mad at first but she said yes. It was that simple. . . . Something wanted to say no when I watched Sally going into the garden with Tito's buddies all grinning. . . . So what, she said. (89)

The socializing and conditioning effect of games is clearly evident in this episode where, pretending to be playing, the boys imitate patriarchal power by setting the rules of the game, and Sally, imitating what she thinks are female means of gaining male approval, passively acquiesces to sexual control. Whereas Esperanza intuits that "something wasn't right" (89), that the boys are violating Sally's natural right over her own body, Sally, having internalized male definitions of her sexuality, sees her own actions as a sign of being a grown-up woman.

In the role she has assumed as the streetwise, grown-up woman, Sally becomes Esperanza's guide to what to her are the secrets of womanhood—how to put on make-up, how to dress—with the implication that Sally also becomes the transmitter of cultural values in respect to how girls are supposed to relate to boys. The initial presentiment, however, that something is wrong in the way the adolescent boys interact with Sally is confirmed when Esperanza, left alone by Sally and her boyfriend in an amusement park, is confronted with male power and sexually attacked by a group of boys. To Esperanza the reality of this brutal sexual initiation stands in sharp contrast to what she has been told about sexual relationships: "Sally, you lied. It

The House on Mango Street   99

wasn't what you said at all. What he did. Where he touched me. I didn't want it, Sally. The way they said it, the way it's supposed to be, all the storybooks and movies, why did you lie to me?" (93).

This last question is central to Esperanza's sexual initiation, as it shows that she feels violated, not only physically by the boys, but also psychologically by a framework of omnipresent cultural myths that shroud the reality of patriarchal violence in idealistic romance. Her disillusionment with the reality of sexual encounters is thus aggravated by her bewilderment as to why "they"—Sally, other women, mass media—have lied to her and left her vulnerable to male sexual advances and domination. As Herrera-Sobek points out, Esperanza's diatribe is directed particularly against the community of women who participate in a "conspiracy of silence": "The protagonist discovers a conspiracy of two forms of silence: silence in not denouncing the 'real' facts of life about sex and its negative aspects in violent sexual encounters, and complicity in embroidering a fairy-tale-like mist around sex" (1988, 178). Thus Esperanza expresses her sense of alienation and betrayal:

> Why did you leave me all alone? I waited my whole life.
> You're a liar. They all lied. All the books and magazines,
> everything that told it wrong. Only his dirty fingernails
> against my skin, only his sour smell again. . . . He wouldn't let
> me go. He said, I love you, I love you, Spanish girl. (94)

Realizing that cultural stories do not tell the whole story, Esperanza condemns this cultural conspiracy around sexuality which—as the depreciatory epithet "Spanish girl" indicates—makes her particularly vulnerable. Esperanza's sexual initiation is thus an initiation into knowledge about herself as a sexual subject who has been manipulated by a framework of cultural myths. By telling her own version of her sexual initiation, however, Esperanza creates a text that stands in direct opposition to the cultural texts, the storybooks, magazines, and movies "that told it wrong," thus refusing to participate in the conspiracy of silence which co-opts women into partaking in their own oppression.

In her attempt to deconstruct socio-cultural lies by telling the truth, Esperanza turns her narrative attention to the women on Mango Street. Realizing that their fate can be hers, she begins to examine their lives in order to come to an understanding of her own relationship to the socio-cultural world of the barrio. Perceived from Esperanza's female perspective, this environment takes on distinct characteristics, in that she, in her evolving consciousness about herself as a woman, becomes increasingly aware of the contradictions between her emerging female self and the circumstances that inform women's lives on Mango Street. It is through a continuous tension between herself and her environment and through her interaction with the women in the barrio, that she becomes aware of the true nature of patriarchal ideology and her own position as a woman within her particular socio-cultural context.

In her adolescent search for role models, Esperanza observes the lives of the women in the neighborhood in order to get some clues to her own future life as a woman. In narrating the stories about these women, Esperanza constructs an image of the women around her that is predominantly one of entrapment and constraint. Women are behind windows, entrapped in their own houses, entrapped in the circumstances that determine their lives as women in a poor Latino barrio. There is Mamacita, who "doesn't come out because she is afraid to speak English" (74); and Rosa Vargas, "who is tired all the time from buttoning and bottling and babying, and who cries every day for the man who left without even leaving a dollar . . . or a note explaining how come" (30); and Minerva, who

> is only a little bit older than me but already she has two kids and a husband who left . . . and keeps leaving. . . . He comes back and sends a big rock through the window. Then he is sorry and she opens the door again. Next week she comes

over black and blue and asks what can she do? . . . Her
mother raised her kids alone and it looks like her daughters
will go that way too. (80)

The women portrayed here exemplify the triple oppression poor
Latino women on Mango Street have to face in their daily lives and
how "women's marginality leads to economic and social dependence
on the male" (Herrera-Sobek, 1988, 175); unable to break the cycle
of poverty or their dependency on men, the daughters are often
doomed to repeat the fate of their mothers.

A common denominator uniting almost all the different women
Esperanza portrays is, not only their entrapment in oppressive socio-
cultural circumstances, but their internalization of a definition of
self that is determined by phallocentric cultural values. They are thus
not only confined within their own houses, but also confined by their
own minds, by the conditioned limitations of their own self-perception. Their lives and actions, dominated by fathers and husbands,
are physically and psychologically entrapped within oppressive patriarchal structures, and they can envision themselves only in the
seemingly inescapable roles of future wives and mothers. Rafaela,
for instance, who "gets locked indoors because her husband is afraid
she will run away since she is too beautiful to look at . . . leans out
the window . . . and dreams her hair is like Rapunzel's" (76), dreams
of being liberated from her prison, but as in the fairy tale, by a man.
And so Rafaela dreams of going dancing where "always there is someone offering sweeter drinks, someone promising to keep them on a
silver string" (76); dreaming of being released of her present impris-
onment, she can only dream of walking into another. This dependency on a man to liberate you from the oppressive circumstances
of your present life also conditions Marin's dreams of the future, of

a real job downtown because that's where the best jobs are,
since you always get to look beautiful and get to wear nice
clothes and can meet someone on the subway who might
marry and take you to live in a big house far away. (27)

Like Esperanza, Marin wants to escape from Mango Street, but unlike Esperanza she envisions marriage as the only possible way of getting away.

It is, however, in her attempt to understand her friend Sally that the narrating "I" begins to see why girls repeat the fate of their marginalized mothers and become caught in a cycle of patriarchal violence and control. Esperanza wants to be beautiful like Sally, dress like Sally, whose father thinks that "to be this beautiful is trouble" (77) and whom the whole world expects "to make a mistake" (79). Yet by narrating Sally's story, she begins to understand that to be Sally also means to end up confined within patriarchal prisons like most of the women on Mango Street.

Sally, who becomes different when she has to go home, cannot leave her house because of her father: "He hits me . . . with his hands just like a dog . . . like if I was an animal. He thinks I'm going to run away like his sisters who made the family ashamed. Just because I'm a daughter" (85). Constant scars on her skin are signs of her father's continuous violent attempts to control her sexuality and force her into adhering to his patriarchal definition of womanhood. This violent drama culminates one day when "he just went crazy, he just forgot he was her father between the buckle and the belt" (85). Making connections between female behavior and patriarchal violence, Esperanza begins to understand why Sally, like Minerva and all the other women on Mango Street, went "that way too" (80) and exchanged her father's prison for that of a husband, believing, like Rafaela, in someone promising to give her "sweeter drinks," to keep her on "a silver string" (76):

> Sally got married like we knew she would, young and not
> ready but married just the same. . . . She has her husband
> and her house now, her pillowcases and her plates. She says
> she is in love, but I think she did it to escape. Sally says she
> likes being married because now she gets to buy her own
> things when her husband gives her money. . . . Except he

won't let her talk on the telephone. And he doesn't let her look out the window. . . . She sits at home because she is afraid to go out without his permission. (96)

Confined physically and psychologically to her house, Sally is trapped in an existence that is completely circumscribed and controlled by her husband; aware of no other alternatives, she leads a life that reflects a recurrent pattern in patriarchal cultural myths, one in which "women do not grow up. They simply change masters—from a beastly father to a fatherly beast" (Rose, 223). Narrating Sally's story, Esperanza comes to understand that, by marrying, Sally remains under the control of a man, and that the house she inhabits, rather than being a liberating space, is a stifling confinement in which Sally is trapped, "looking at walls, the linoleum roses on the floor, the ceiling smooth as a wedding cake" (95). She is, in effect, trapped between the myth and the reality of women's lives.

Sally's house stands as an antithesis to the house Esperanza dreams of inhabiting one day; it is also a far cry from Gaston Bachelard's image of a house as "felicitous space" (xxxv), or Tomás Rivera's definition of *la casa* as a "constant refuge" (1979, 22) from a hostile world. In Bachelard's reveries, a house is "the non-I that protects the I" (5), "a roomy home" where a family can live "in security and comfort" (30), where one shivers "merely from well-being" (31). He deems this experience of the house as a "material paradise" (7) to be so universal that it can be used as "a tool for analysis of the human soul" (xxxvii). It is obvious that this image of the house has its roots in Bachelard's own comfortable background and that his reveries on the house are circumscribed by a male-centered middle-class ideology. His "nostalgic and privileged utopia" (Olivares, 160) is based on experiences that differ dramatically from those of women like Sally and Esperanza.

There is a marked economic and cultural difference between Bachelard's concept of the house as "material paradise" and Tomás Rivera's concept of *la casa* as a "constant refuge" (1979, 22) from a

Bildung as a Subversive Act

hostile environment. In his article "Fiesta of the Living," Rivera presents *la casa, el barrio,* and *la lucha* as constant and essential elements in the struggle for cultural survival in a hostile environment. To Rivera, *la casa* is the center of cultural continuity, a safe haven where ethnic pride and family solidarity are perpetuated. Central to this concept of *la casa* is also the image of the much eulogized *madre abnegada,* who sacrifices herself for her family. This concept of the traditional family may perpetuate ethnic integrity and mitigate the blows of oppression, but for the Chicana it may also be the very concept that perpetuates her own oppression. Despite their differences, both Bachelard and Rivera see the house as a protective sphere, "the non-I that protects the I," a concept that does not always apply to women, as it is often within the very confines of the home that violence is visited upon her. To Sally, the house is neither a "material paradise" nor a "constant refuge"; in order to escape the physical violence in her father's house, she marries, only to realize that she has exchanged one prison for another.

Esperanza comes to realize, in examining the lives of the women on Mango Street, that a woman's house is often a confining patriarchal domain rather than the house of liberation she imagines for herself. Having arrived at this realization, Esperanza begins to resist the social conditioning that leads women on the path to marriage:

> My mother says when I get older my dusty hair will settle
> and my blouse will learn to stay clean, but I have decided not
> to grow up tame like the others who lay their necks on the
> threshold waiting for the ball and chain. I have begun my
> own quiet war. Simple. Sure. I am one who leaves the table
> like a man, without putting back the chair or picking up the
> plate. (82)

Esperanza's refusal to adhere to social expectations of female behavior goes far beyond the mere action itself, as it is a symbolic refusal to "grow up tame," to accept a prescribed female destiny. Esperanza's action has been interpreted as a "somewhat adolescent gesture" that is likely "to increase the work for another woman in Esperanza's household" (McCracken, 72) and as an attempt "to increase her own power by starting out to be as rude as men" (Alarcón, 1989, 100), yet her refusal to do so-called female chores marks an important step toward breaking the cycle of female self-sacrifice. With her self-defining assertions, "I have decided not to grow up tame . . . , I am one who leaves the table," Esperanza claims control over her own *Bildungs* process by envisioning a role for herself that stands in direct opposition to the socio-cultural roles and expectations imposed on women by a male-defined culture. In her own "quiet war," Esperanza begins to assert a self-defined destiny by "daring to be selfish" (Huf, 157), by daring to kill the "angel in the house" (Woolf, 1942, 236), so that she can inhabit her own liberating space, a house of her own making:

> Not a flat. Not an apartment in the back. Not a man's house. Not a daddy's. A house all my own. With my porch and pillow, my pretty purple petunias. My books and my stories. My two shoes waiting besides the bed. Nobody to shake a stick at. Nobody's garbage to pick up after. Only a house as quiet as snow, a space for myself to go, clean as paper before the poem. (100)

Her initial wish for an illusive "real house," one she can point to, is thus in the course of her narrative transformed into a more defined desire for a place that transcends the mere physical living quarters to mean a life of her own creation. She wants not only a house but also a life that is unconfined by either a father or a husband or prescriptive social expectations, a nonpatriarchal space in which she can create herself and a self-defined destiny.

In the process of her exploration of her socio-cultural context, of discovering, synthesizing, and narrating her own experiences within the community on Mango Street, Esperanza has come to understand that the "real house" she has been searching for is an unconfining creative space. Telling her own story, the narrating "I" participates in the process of her own self-formation, while she at the same time creates a poetic space that stands as an alternative to the confining conditions on Mango Street: "I like to tell stories. . . . I put it down on paper and then the ghost does not ache so much. I write it down and Mango Street says goodbye sometimes. She does not hold me with both arms. She sets me free" (101). This sense of liberation through the creative act of writing and narrating her own stories is predicted early on by a dying aunt who encourages Esperanza to write: "'That's nice. That's very good,' she said in her tired voice. 'You just remember to keep writing, Esperanza. You must keep writing. It will keep you free,' and I said, 'yes,' but at that time I didn't know what she meant" (56). Attention here turns to the narrating "I," who, through the creative reconstruction of this encounter, comes to understand that in writing about her experiences she has come to inhabit a liberating poetic space of her own.

Esperanza's vision of creativity as a form of liberation takes on social and cultural dimensions, as it becomes clear that *The House on Mango Street* is the narrator/author's textual return to Mango Street. The narrating "I," initially ashamed of her entire "social and subject position" (Saldívar, 1990, 182), is driven throughout the narrative process by the desire to escape not only her great-grandmother's "place by the window," but also the confinement of her socio-economic circumstances on Mango Street. Yet in the course of telling her stories she comes to recognize the significance of Mango Street in her life, that it forms an inextricable part of her own self.

In the course of her *Bildung*, Esperanza encounters several guides, each of whom connects her with her cultural context in vital ways and provides important messages about the uniqueness of her own identity. There is her mother who "could've been somebody" (83) if it had not been for the shame of being poor: "Shame is a bad thing, you know. It keeps you down. You want to know why I quit school?

Because I didn't have nice clothes. No clothes, but I had brains" (84). That the feeling of shame can entrap one in the very situation one wants to escape becomes a crucial lesson for Esperanza, who, throughout the narrative, has expressed being ashamed of her position on Mango Street. Her friend Alicia, furthermore, insists that Mango Street, the very place Esperanza wants to escape, forms an integral part of Esperanza's identity: "Like it or not you are Mango Street and one day you will come back" (99). This emphasis on her connection to Mango Street is reiterated by three *comadres,* three indigenous guides—reminiscent of the three Fates in Greek mythology who govern human destiny—who tell her that she is "special," that she will "go far" (97), but also that she must not forget that she comes from Mango Street:

> Esperanza . . . a good, good name.
> When you leave you must remember always to come back, she said. . . . When you leave you must remember to come back for the others. A circle, understand? You will always be Esperanza. You will always be Mango Street. You can't erase what you know: You can't forget who you are. You must remember to come back. For the ones who cannot leave as easily as you.
> Yes, yes, I said a little confused.
> I didn't understand everything they had told me. (98)

Once more the attention turns to the narrating "I" who, through the creative reconstruction of her life on Mango Street, has come to understand that she will always be Esperanza. She will always be a Chicana, and Mango Street will always form a part of her identity. The *comadres* predict a different destiny for Esperanza, yet remind her at the same time that her origins, her cultural and socio-economic roots, form an important part of her future self. When Esperanza in the end envisions her own departure from Mango Street, it is with the intention of returning, of creating *esperanza* for those she leaves behind:

One day I will pack my bags of books and paper. One day I will say goodbye to Mango. I am too strong for her to keep me here forever. One day I will go away.

Friends and neighbors will say, What happened to that Esperanza? Where did she go with all those books and paper? Why did she march so far away? They will not know that I have gone away to come back. For the ones I left behind. For the ones who cannot get out. (102)

By the end of her *Bildungs* experience, Esperanza has thus gained an awareness of herself as a potential writer who ventures into the larger world with a firm sense of who she is, where she comes from, and where she is going.

The House on Mango Street is a narrative of self-discovery in which Esperanza narrates her own quest for a house, a life of her own making. Through the act of narrating, the Chicana protagonist becomes the conscious subject of her own *Bildungs* story. She is a female *Bildungsheld* who dismantles "the cultural text as she grows up in resistance to it" (J. Frye, 109), resisting cultural norms that demand that women "grow down rather than up" (Pratt, 1981, 168). In the process she creates a text that subverts the traditional female quest story of the "thwarted or impossible journey" (Heller, 14) that inevitably leads to socio-cultural entrapment of the female hero. Narrating her own *Bildungs* story, the narrating "I" engages in the subversive act of replacing the cultural text with her own. This aspect of the narrative lends a poetic dimension to this Chicana quest story: Esperanza's search for a "real" house is at the same time a quest for self-expression, for a liberating self-creation that dismantles traditional male-defined myths and texts that have locked the Chicana into confining stereotypes.

When Esperanza at the end of her self-discovering narrative envisions the "real" house she has been searching for, she defines it as "not a man's house. Not a daddy's. A house all my own. . . . A house quiet as snow, a space for myself to go, clean as paper before the poem" (100). This connection between the house and the text—her house is a poem yet to be written—turns her rejection of a "man's house" into a rejection of what Gilbert and Gubar have termed "patriarchal poetics" (72); her escape from the house of the fathers is an escape from male texts. Her own quest for a "real" house is thus a quest for a new Chicana text, one that names her own experiences and represents her as a Chicana in all her subjective complexity, one that does not make her "feel like nothing."

This use of the house as a metaphor for a new Chicana poetic space is further underscored by Esperanza's image of her own house as a place of ethnic consciousness and with room for outsiders: "One day I'll own my own house, but I won't forget who I am or where I came from. Passing bums will ask, Can I come in? I'll offer them the attic, ask them to stay, because I know how it is to be without a house" (81). Esperanza's house/text, the poem that is yet to be written, is thus going to include the traditional outsiders, the socio-cultural "others," who have been excluded from inhabiting houses/texts of their own. And in fact, many of these "others" inhabit the finished text, *The House on Mango Street,* as for example Geraldo, who did not have a last name, who was "just another *brazer* who didn't speak English. Just another wetback. You know the kind. The ones who always look ashamed" (63). By making room for the story of a *mojado* in her text, Esperanza gives poetic space to one of the many outsiders who otherwise sink into oblivion, nameless and forgotten.

The House on Mango Street is a text that houses outsiders, where those who look ashamed because they do not have houses/texts of their own can feel at home. It is a concern that may stem from Cisneros's own feelings of textual exclusion. In a biographical essay, Sandra Cisneros recalls her encounter with Gaston Bachelard's *The Poetry of Space* in college. She did not understand Bachelard's reveries on the house of the imagination, yet everyone else was quite comfortable with this book, and that made her feel "foreign from the others, out of place, different" (63):

> They seemed to have some communal knowledge which I did not have, did not understand—and then I realized that the metaphor of the *house* was totally wrong for me, that it did not draw from any archetype in my imagination, in my past culture. Suddenly I was homeless. There were no attics, and cellars, and crannies. I had no such house in my memories. (63)

Cisneros's feelings of homelessness in Bachelard's text stem from her inability to relate to a concept of the house that is based on a male-centered, middle-class ideology that is foreign to her. Bachelard's "felicitous space" finds no echo in Cisneros's imagination, and the house of her childhood was not the "material paradise" (7) that Bachelard seems to presume is a universal given. *The House on Mango Street* is thus a countertext to Bachelard's *The Poetics of Space*, a Chicana poetics of space that houses images which reverberate in the Chicana imagination. With *The House on Mango Street*, Cisneros has created a text that, unlike Bachelard's text, can house the imagination of the textual outsider.

Much in keeping with Esperanza's promise to return for the women she leaves behind, "the ones who cannot get out" (102), *The House on Mango Street* stands as a symbolic return to the women in a Latino barrio. Not only is this Chicana *Bildungsroman* dedicated "A las Mujeres/To the Women," but the narrative itself centers on the community of women on Mango Street who form part of Esperanza's *Bildungs* process. Elsewhere Sandra Cisneros argues that "the world of thousands of silent women . . . needs to be, must be recorded so that their stories can finally be heard" (76). Through the narrator/protagonist, Esperanza, Sandra Cisneros gives voice to a Chicana *Bildungsheld* who tells her own story, who in the process of constructing herself as a subject "dares to confront lies and to deconstruct myths" (Gonzales-Berry, 14) about la Chicana.

Esperanza grows up, not down, and gains in the process a clear understanding of her social, cultural, and sexual identity as a Chicana. Through her role as a writer, as a teller of stories, however, her *Bildung* is not merely individual, but takes on communal significance, as she, with the text, is reaching back to the women on Mango Street so that her own liberating self-creation may in turn become a symbolic *Bildungs* experience for those "who cannot get out":

Marin, under the streetlight, dancing by herself, is singing the same song somewhere. I know. Is waiting for a car to stop, a star to fall, someone to change her life. Anybody. (28)

The communal significance of Esperanza's *Bildung* is further underscored by the fact that, while her primary concern is for the women who cannot escape marginalization, the text goes beyond an exclusive portrayal of the oppression of Chicanas to name and give voice to other outsiders in the community. *The House on Mango Street* thus exemplifies how Esperanza's *Bildung* involves an understanding of her own relationship to the entire Chicano community and that such understanding is essential to a true Chicana *Bildungs* process.

4

THE LAST OF THE MENU GIRLS
Learning from the Women

*And several things nobody knows about me. But in the end it's important we
each tell our versions, set the story straight and write our own interpretations
instead of having them written for us. Sometimes one needs to reinvent one's
past before one can re-invent one's future.*

—SANDRA CISNEROS

The Last of the Menu Girls (1986) by Denise Chávez consists of
seven interrelated sections narrated by Rocío Esquibel, the female
protagonist who recollects her own adolescent rites of passage, the
dreams and experiences that formed part of her passage into womanhood. Set in a Chicano barrio in southern New Mexico during the
early sixties, *The Last of the Menu Girls* portrays everyday events and
experiences that form part of Rocío's life among her own extended
family, *comadres* and *compadres,* neighbors and friends. It is in this
bicultural and bilingual border milieu that Rocío begins to examine
her own relationship to her environment, look for role models, and
examine the lives of the women around her in search of her own
identity, her own self. Telling her own story, the narrating "I" remem-
bers her adolescent years and, in the process of her narrative reconstruction of her past, she gives pattern and meaning to those ordinary
events and daily relationships that informed her own *Bildungs* process.
The narrative focus on her own subjective experiences allows Rocío
to affirm her origins and at the same time subvert external defini-

tions of herself. Through the act of remembering, Rocío claims her past, creating meaning out of a mosaic of past experiences and impressions, all of which form a part of her Chicana identity. *The Last of the Menu Girls* is peopled mainly by women who are caught in the bitter reality of lost hopes and broken dreams. Nevertheless, the narrator/protagonist is able to imagine herself beyond that reality in her desire to become a Chicana writer who is able to interpret and re-create her own past in a creative affirmation of her cultural origins. By returning to the symbolic world of her childhood and adolescence, the narrator's reconstruction of her own *Bildungs* process becomes at the same time a search for her roots as a writer; remembering her quest for an authentic self, she also re-creates her own search for a creative voice.

It is, perhaps, not surprising that this *Bildungsroman* begins with a reference to the link between self and nature. Going back to her early years, the narrative "I" recalls her childhood world, marked off by trees and full of familiar faces:

> I was a child before there was a South. That was before the
> magic of the East, the beckoning North, or the West's
> betrayal. For me there was simply Up the street toward the
> spies' house, next to Old Man W's or there was Down, past
> the Marking-Off Tree in the vacant lot that was the shortcut
> between worlds. Down was the passageway to family, the
> definition of small self as one of the whole, part of a past. (41)

Still unaware of the socio-political and cultural implications of her own region and its relationship to the rest of the country, Rocío passes her childhood within the protective range of three familiar trees that mark off "the nearest point home, without being home" (44). This is her imaginary world of play and fantasy. Living in a world full of women, Rocío perceives these trees as female, and sees them as a symbolic extension of her own household. With time two of the trees wither away. The third tree, however, the Willow Tree, is slowly mutilated to death by a destructive Anglo boy next door. This act, which stands as a symbolic male violation of what to Rocío signifies a natural, female sphere, coincides with an archetypal pattern in women's fiction in which nature represents "freedom, solace, and protection" to the adolescent girl, and men are pictured as "agents of harsh disruption" of a protective green world (Pratt, 1981, 25). With the trees gone, Rocío's green world, the protective shield these trees offered the world of her childhood innocence, disappears. Although her mother plants a new willow tree to return their environment to its familiar state, Rocío's childhood innocence cannot be restored: "I am left with recollections of pain, of loss, with holes to be filled. . . . The shreds of magic living, like the silken, green ropes of the Willow's branches, dissolved about me, and I was beyond myself, a child no longer." (49-50)

The house, Rocío's home, is a central metaphor throughout the novel. It is a house full of memories of the past, of Great Aunt Eutilia who died, of her mother's first husband who was poisoned, and her own father who left to go north. It is a house where "the old shaving lotion was a reminder that we lived in a house of women" (86). Full of obsolete objects and mementos of a past her mother wants to preserve and remember, the house forms an integral part of the family: "I love this house, your daddy built this house, you were born here, and we've lived here ever since, this house is fifteen years old and it's full of *us*, our things" (140). It is here that Rocío, no longer a child and eager to be initiated into the mysteries of women's lives, becomes aware of the fact that Nieves is not only her mother, but also a woman with a past, with dreams and desires of her own. As a way of gaining an understanding of her own identity as a woman, she begins to explore the house to get to know the woman who is her mother.

The closets of the house constitute the very heart of the house. They correspond to the interior, secret life of her mother that forms part of Rocío's memories and shapes her own concept of self. The closets represent a vast field for exploration, "time and fantasy and dreams" (89), and they "lead into the heart and spirit of the house" (91) and of the people who lived there. It is in her mother's closet that Rocío begins to know the other side of her mother's life. It is here, among old, hidden photographs and worn out shoes, that she begins to piece together her mother's story:

> In the half-tone darkness my eyes travel from the wedding photograph at the back of the closet to the reality of my mother's other life. Shoes crowd the floor. . . . They are the shoes of a woman with big feet, tired legs, furious bitter hopes. They are the shoes of someone who has stood all her life in line waiting for better things to come. (79)

Wedding photographs show a younger, happier version of her mother; hidden behind piles of clothes, they are the remnants of a happiness that lasted only one year. Venturing into the secret corners of her mother's closet, Rocío encounters other remnants of a past "sacred and off-limits"—"photographs, articles of clothing, papers" (88)—bits and pieces of a life spent with unfulfilled hopes. Here Rocío finds the reality of her mother's "other life," "the smell of my mother's loneliness" (80). Her mother's only wish is to have a man around the house, "someone like my father," a man with "the ability to do, to fix, to lift, to support and to think through" (169). Although Nieves is raising her daughters on her own, she is still psychologically dependent on a man, describing her own life without a husband as a "very hard, a painful life" (170).

Rocío's attempt to get to know her mother as a person is indicative of the importance of the relationship between mother and daughter in a woman's *Bildungs* process and the formation of her female identity. In a patriarchal context, however, the relationship between mother and daughter is charged with ambiguities, because accepting the mother as a role model may signify accepting oppressive, socially prescribed norms of womanhood. The mother often embodies a female identity the daughter refuses to assume. This ambiguous situation makes the female process of individuation particularly difficult:

> For a girl, becoming a woman means assuming the sex of her mother, to whom society offers few rewards and whose own self-esteem is consequently often low. Even if the daughter likes the mother personally, she may dislike her mother's role and rebel against assuming a similar position. (Stewart, 42)

Just as Esperanza in *The House on Mango Street* did not want to inherit her great-grandmother's place by the window, so Rocío does not want to inherit her mother's place in the line "waiting for better things to come" (79), the enclosure of the female self that her mother's closet represents. Thus, while her mother seeks solace in the memories of a life that could have been, and whose memorabilia are now locked up in a closet, Rocío ventures beyond the enclosure of her mother's life to imagine her own future.

In an attempt to distance herself from the confinement of her mother's life and find an alternative to the world of her mother's closets, Rocío begins to create her own imaginary "closets," the Grey Room and the Blue Room, rooms that are all her own and where she imagines herself free to fly. This imaginary flight into a space of her own indicates a growing desire to escape confinement and manifest a self-defined identity. Trying to explain this imaginary world to her younger sister, Rocío echoes Virginia Woolf in her insistence that everybody has to have "their *own* rooms, their *own* house" (93). In other words, one has to have a space where one can imagine oneself into being. Thus, while her mother seeks solace in her memories, Rocío creates an imaginary world of her own, where she can be herself and imagine her own future self somewhere beyond her mother's fate.

As Rocío grows older and begins to struggle with her own emerging identity as a woman, she also begins to distance herself from the house and what it represents to her: "*Everything* is wrong! Everything! I hate this house it's so junky and messy and crammed full of crap. . . . It's crowded and dusty and dark. . . . I just wish it would burn down so we could start all over again!" (140). Much as her mother is protective of her house, her memories, and her past, so Rocío's rejection of the house manifests an emerging self that feels suffocated by a house full of relics of her mother's past. Rocío wants to start anew, liberate herself from the house and all it represents in order to shape her own identity. With an increasing awareness of the developmental process she is going through, Rocío becomes the "solitary observer" (62) of her changing womanhood and of her own quest for a viable self: "I was looking for someone. Someone. That someone, Myself" (158).

Rocío's world is indeed a world of women. Surrounded by female relatives of several generations—sisters, grandmothers, *comadres,* aunts, cousins—Rocío becomes increasingly aware that she forms part of this extended family of women. When she, for instance, as a child creates her own imaginary rooms, she also imagines being visited by the spirits of female relatives who express their love for her. Her childhood vacations in Texas are likewise remembered as summers spent among laughing women, sharing family anecdotes. Rocío's father, an infrequent visitor from up north, exists only on the margins of her life without exerting any influence on any of the family members. This family of women suggests a restructuring of the traditional patriarchal family on the part of the author that coincides with Ortega and Sternbach's observation that Latina writers often displace "a central patriarchal figure, replacing it with a woman-headed and woman-populated household" (13). With the father removed from Rocío's environment, the author has removed the father-daughter conflict in order to focus the narrative attention on cross-generational female relationships and their influence on Rocío's self-formation.

It is within this female sphere of older and younger women that Rocío becomes aware of the different cycles that form a part of a

Bildung as Subversive Act

woman's life as well as the physical effect of aging. Wondering about her own future as a woman and examining the women around her from that perspective, she sees women of the older generation defined by physical suffering and pain. If the women on Mango Street were locked into their houses by their husbands, here Rocío perceives elderly women to be locked into the gradual decay of their own bodies. This aspect of human life provokes an aversion in Rocío. Her dislike originates, perhaps, with her experiences at home with her great-aunt, whose odors of bodily decay, suffering, and gradual dying left a lasting impression on her memory. Her predominantly female environment is, furthermore, full of stories about female physical suffering, as, for instance, the one about Doña Mercedes, who died of cancer:

When the young women went to lift the old lady from her death bed, they struggled to pull her from the sheets; and, when finally they turned her on her side, they saw huge gaping holes in her back where the cancer had eaten through the flesh. The sheets were stained, the bedsores lost in a red wash of bloody pus. (17)

Stories like this one, together with her own experiences at home, make Rocío associate physical illness and decay with women and fear a similar fate: "I never wanted to be like Great Aunt Eutilia, or Doña Mercedes with the holes in her back, or my mother, her scarred legs, her whitened thighs" (17). When she later gets a work-study job in a hospital, Rocío is confronted with more women ravaged by "deep hurts, deep distresses" (30), women who make her see herself in them, "all life, all suffering. What I saw both chilled and burned me" (27).

This reiterated and explicit attention to female disease goes beyond the mere physical aspects of illness to become a metaphor for what Rocío perceives to be the "infected" nature of women's lives. Rocío's aversion to female disease is at the same time a repulsion by a debilitating female destiny that locks women into norms and roles which stand in direct opposition to what she imagines for her own future. Confronted with female situations she rejects, Rocío voices a desire to leave, to escape the destiny of the women around her, whom she sees as victims of not only their own bodies, but also of their condition as women: "I want to be someone else, somewhere else" (34). Rocío at seventeen, "too afraid to linger, too unwilling to see," aware of her own budding womanhood, her own sexuality, is confronted with female fates and destinies that terrify her, yet looking back she recognizes that these experiences were central to her own development: "I had made that awesome leap into myself that steamy summer of illness and dread—confronting at every turn, the flesh, its lingering cries" (35–36). If Rocío wants to escape the house and closet of her mother, she also wants to escape a debilitating female destiny that would prevent her from achieving authentic selfhood.

With "awkward limbs, uncertain dreams" (70), Rocío begins to search for the woman she is to become, to wonder about the nature of womanhood: "What did it mean to be a woman? To be beautiful, complete? Was beauty a physical or a spiritual thing, was it strength of emotion, resolve, a willingness to love? What was it then, that made women lovely?" (53). To find some answers to these questions, she begins to examine the women around her in search of someone she can pattern herself on, someone who can serve as her role model. To Rocío, her friends Eloise, Diana, and Josie represent physical and spiritual female beauty, each of them the embodiment of the mystery of what makes a woman desired and loved. Yet each of them falls short of what she imagines to be her own future womanhood.

One of these women, the beautiful Eloise, admits Rocío into her "magical woman's world" (56) and is Rocío's revered image of immaculate perfection, like an "immutable, unnamed virgin" (56), until the day she sees a smoking Eloise "chortling and braying like a rude goat" in the company of a man who has "his paws across her shoulder" (56). The man is portrayed not only as the disrupter of a female union, but as a beastly male force who exerts his power over the young female. Eloise accepts his possessive "paw," acquiesces to be possessed, which to Rocío amounts to an act of betrayal of female selfhood. Rocío, having been caught up in a romantic notion of the ideal woman, is here confronted with the other aspect of that role that requires female assent to patriarchal domination.

Another potential role model, Diana, is, as opposed to Eloise, "fresh, bright-eyed, hopeful and kind" (57–58), the embodiment of selfless femininity. However, as Rocío gets to know her better, she discovers a naive, inarticulate girl, whose thoughts are "confused, jangled, unsure," someone who is lost in "half syllables, monosyllabic utterings" (58). Diana's inarticulateness, her confusion about language, forms part of her femininity and indicates her internalization of prescribed feminine shortcomings, what Gilbert and Gubar call "a sort of intellectual incapacity patriarchal culture has traditionally required of women" (58). Her silence represents "the unnatural thwarting of what struggles to come into being, but cannot" (Olsen, 6), a muted selfhood that is deterred from self-definition by the internalization of the feelings of self-doubt and inferiority that her female conditioning has produced. Recalling her fascination for Diana and her subsequent disappointment, the narrating "I" comments on her own quest for a viable self: "In observing Diana, I observed myself. I wanted physical beauty, and yet, I wanted to speak clearly, to be understood" (58). It becomes clear that language, the capacity for self-expression, is intimately connected to identity. Rocío's search for self goes beyond the external definitions of womanhood to a subjectivity that can be defined through the language of others; her desire to "speak clearly" is the initial creative urge for self-definition of the emerging writer choosing her own language.

After having discarded Eloise and Diana as possible role models, Rocío continues her speculations about the mysteries of womanhood and, still left with unanswered questions, she turns to Josie for clues to her own uncertain future as a woman. Josie, with black spike heels and plunging necklines, the center of attention at every party, is the embodiment of feminine beauty, of Rocío's "womanly hopes" (61). Admiring her beauty and her popularity, however, Rocío also realizes that Josie is one of a species of "charming, vibrant, effusive bird creatures, caught and trapped in lovely, shiny cages" (62), caught, that is, in a prescribed feminine identity. Performing her role as a beautiful object and finding self-affirmation only in the eyes of those she wants to please, Josie is defined and confined by external definitions of herself.

Each of these three women follows prescribed female roles, and although they at first are perceived to be the embodiment of the adolescent Rocío's "womanly hopes," each of them falls short of what she imagines to be her own future self: "Who was I, then to choose as model? . . . Something seemed to be lacking in each of them. The same thing that was lacking in me, whatever it was" (62). What is lacking in each of these women is the authenticity of a self-defined identity, the affirmation of selfhood Rocío is searching for. This difficulty in finding a suitable role model illustrates Barbara White's argument that "adolescent heroines would no doubt find it easier to grow up female if they could admire and identify with adult women. However, the girls seldom want to pattern themselves after any of the women they know" (141). Through her emerging comprehension of the world and her growing self-awareness, Rocío realizes that she cannot use any of the women she knows as a model for her future self. Caught in the confusion of her own development as a woman, however, she begins to imagine a future self who, through creative self-expression, will be able to gain an understanding of her own *Bildungs* process: "Perhaps someday when I grow older . . . maybe then I can recollect and recount the real significance of things in a past as elusive as clouds passing" (57).

In her futile search for a potential role model, however, Rocío makes an important discovery, in that she begins to recognize her

Bildung as Subversive Act

own place in a long line of women. Although she rejects becoming like her mother or other female relatives, watching their features, their bodies, she begins to recognize herself in them:

> It was my sister's pores, her postures that were my teachers, her flesh, with and without clothes, that was my awakening, and her face that was the mirror image of my growing older. To see her, was to see my mother and my grandmother, and now myself. (63)

Rocío thus comes to recognize a matrilineal heritage that situates her firmly within a cultural and historical context. This discovery marks a turning point in her developmental process, as she realizes that her female relatives form an integral part of her female identity. Whereas before she had searched for external role models, she now turns her attention to her own emerging self and finds the first signs of the woman she has been searching for. "Behind all the work of growing up, I caught a glimpse of someone strong, full of great beauty, powerful, clear words and acts. . . . Who was that woman? Myself" (63).

Central to a *Bildungs* process is the interaction between the protagonist and the world, the protagonist's response to her particular environment. This relationship to the socio-cultural environment is particularly important to the Chicana *Bildungsheld,* as it is within the Chicano community that she finds support and protection vis-à-vis an oppressive Anglo world. Thus the community in which Rocío comes of age plays a central role in her process of self-development, as it is through her relationship to this particular socio-cultural context that she gains an understanding of her personal and cultural identity.

Throughout her childhood and adolescence, Rocío is surrounded by people who connect her with her culture in vital ways and provide her with an understanding of her own cultural identity. It is, however, her mother who is the central transmitter of cultural values in Rocío's life. It is she who, for instance, implants in Rocío the importance of the code of *compadrazgo* and *comadrazgo* in their daily lives, the interdependence between godfathers and godmothers that, according to her, is "truer than family, higher than marriage, nearest of all relationships to the balanced, supportive, benevolent universal godhead" (169). With *compadrazgo/comadrazgo* comes the obligation to help your *compadre* or *comadre*. A case in point is Regino. A Mexican handyman who does slipshod work, the mother hires him nevertheless, knowing that he needs the work; she furthermore helps him with his large family, feeling responsible for their well-being. Here the mother takes on the role of *la patrona*, who, although she does not have much money, feels a responsibility toward members of the community who have even less. The mother is very conscious of her own status in the community and that the well-being of others depends on her benevolence.

The code of *compadrazgo* is a code of mutual support and mutual responsibility. Just as the *madrina*, the godmother, should always be ready to provide "a home, warm clothes, and food" for the *ahijado*, the godchild, so the *madrina* or *padrino*, the godfather or godmother, should never be forgotten:

> God help the ahijado, if he forgets who his madrina or
> padrino is. They're your one phone call and you'd better not
> forget that number, you remember that, Rocío. You could be
> left relationless, and what could be worse than that? You'd be
> disconnected from any living soul, unable to say 'tío, tía or
> hermano.' (168)

According to the mother the worst fate that could befall Rocío is to become relationless, without the support and affection of the extended family system. These cultural values the mother passes on to her daughter situate Rocío within an extended network of relationships that connect her to the community and give her a sense of responsibility toward the community. Growing up within this context of communal relationships, Rocío thus learns to see her own identity as firmly related to a community that forms part of who she is and where she comes from.

It is when Rocío ventures beyond her community that she begins to hear conflicting voices about cultural identity and ethnic relations in her environment. At the hospital where she has a work-study job, "that place of white women and whiter men with square faces" (17), she witnesses the arrival of a Mexican who has had his nose bitten off in a barroom brawl. His arrival provokes a revealing discussion among the personnel about the so-called "epidemic" of "illegal aliens" from Mexico and the way they are treated. Although some feel sorry for the man, the main tenet of the discussion is expressed by Esperanza, a nurse who rails against "the Anglo sons of bitches and at all the lousy wetbacks," and against outsiders who, according to her, don't understand the situation: "You just leave these alien problems to those of us who were brought up around here and know what's going on. . . . Christ, . . . what do you expect, he don't speak no Engleesh!" (33). Only Rocío seems to see him, not as an illegal alien, but as an individual human being with his own identity: "His name is Juan María Mejía" (33). The nurse, however, is not interested in his identity. Feeling caught in the middle between Anglos and "wetbacks," she has no compassion or responsibility for undocumented immigrants and has a clear view of her own role in respect to the problems the border represents: "We're just here to clean up the mess" (32). This Chicana thus draws a sharp line between undocumented workers and herself that negates any cultural ties she may have to the country south of the border. Furthermore, having internalized the dominant ideology, she sees these immigrants as an economic threat—"It's a disgrace all those wetbacks and healthy college students getting our hard earned tax money" (36)—a viewpoint that is reiterated by Rocío's father, who, on a short visit, is surprised to see where *compadre* Regino lives: "How long have the wetbacks been allowed up there on the hill? . . . Christ, it pays to be on welfare" (179). These perceptions of Mexican immigrants stand in direct opposition to the communal values of mutual support Rocío has been taught in the barrio. There, as with Rocío's relation to Regino, cultural ties and traditional values prevail over questions of provenance or economic interests. Recalling these incidents, the narrating "I" indicates how she as an adolescent began to become aware of her own subject position as a Chicana from the border, poised between two cultures, two different worldviews, and the multiple social, cultural, and economic implications of that identity.

It is, however, when Rocío leaves home to go to college that she experiences the antithesis to her own barrio context of mutual support and understanding. Recalling her college experience, Rocío portrays a period of complete alienation, where, because nobody can pronounce it, even her name is changed to Miss E ; her landlady, for instance, first thinks Rocío is Filipino, then takes to calling her Spanish. This general inability to pronounce her name is indicative of an environment that is unable or unwilling to recognize her identity as a Chicana. Thus alienated, Rocío seems unable to communicate with anyone or find human support and understanding anywhere. Without money, constantly tired, unable to eat or pay her rent, and dreaming of being surrounded by human impostors, she is finally driven to the brink of a nervous breakdown.

It is significant that in the section "Space is a Solid," which covers this experience of alienation, the narrative breaks up into the individual voices of the landlady, her daughter, Rocío, and Loudon, her boyfriend. These are the voices of people Rocío interacts with on a daily basis, yet people who do not help her or feel responsible for her well-being. Her racist and money grabbing landlady, for instance, does not have any qualms about leaving Rocío in the street when she cannot pay the rent; at the theater, where she works, they threaten to fire her because her landlady, a sponsor of the theater, has complained about her; and Loudon, in turn, does not understand what is wrong with her. Rocío comments on her boyfriend's inability to understand her situation:

> Loudon doesn't understand. I have no home. I am homeless. Where can I move? Why won't Loudon let me stay with him? After all, we are friends. We're *friends,* aren't we? He's too busy, all his time taken up. . . . I don't have a place to live, Loudon doesn't want me, he's told me so. (107)

The voices of both Rocío and the people in her surroundings are voices in conflict, voices that threaten her self-perception and express worldviews and values that stand in opposition to Rocío's own cultural values. The indifference Rocío encounters in her surroundings provokes a deep sense of alienation, the state of disconnectedness her mother had warned would be the worst possible fate to befall her. It is through these experiences that she recognizes the importance of the Chicano community in her quest for identity, and this realization becomes a catalyst for her development as a writer. When Rocío later asks her students in a drama appreciation class to write a story, it becomes clear that her own process of re-creating her past has begun: "Now while you're writing *your* stories, I'll write *mine*" (136); by writing, she begins to "recollect and recount the real significance of things in the past" (57), to re-create her own subjective experiences in order to better understand herself.

At the end of *The Last of the Menu Girls,* Rocío has returned home as a writer. "Yes, I said, I write. I'm a writer" who writes "about people. New Mexico. You know, everything" (190). It is significant that it is her mother who encourages Rocío to write about the community, to write the story of their lives:

> I say, Rocío, just write about this little street of ours, it's only one block long, but there's so many stories. Too many stories! And then I thought to myself, but why write about this street? . . . Why not just write about 325? That's our house! Write about 325 and that will take the rest of your life. . . . There's stories, plenty of them all around. (190)

With *The Last of the Menu Girls* Rocío makes a symbolic return to her roots to recollect and re-create her own rites of passage into womanhood, and through the act of re-creation, to complete her quest for her own identity: "Going back is going forward" (75). And by going back she has come of age as a Chicana writer who through her creativity has found her identity as a woman, as a Chicana and as a writer within the Chicano community.

Both *The House on Mango Street* and *The Last of the Menu Girls* portray a female *Bildungs* process that deviates significantly from the traditional female quest story in that the Chicana protagonist takes on narrative authority over her own experiences, her own *Bildungs* story. Each narrative is thus grounded in the protagonist's conscious exploration of the contradictions between internal and external definitions of the self, between socio-cultural values and gender role expectations and the female self. The narrating "I" articulates her own experiential perspectives on her own *Bildungs* process, and becomes, through the act of articulation, an active agent of her own self-education. The central theme of each narrative is thus the narrator/protagonist's articulation of her own growing consciousness of her position as a woman within her particular socio-cultural context, an understanding that enables each protagonist to imagine herself beyond patriarchal confinement of the female self. If Valentina and Trini in the end succumb to socio-cultural expectations, then Esperanza and Rocío, representing a new generation of Chicanas, gain authenticity and selfhood by openly opposing such entrapment in prescribed female roles and by imagining different ways of being in the world. By shaping and narrating her own *Bildungs* story, the Chicana protagonist claims a subjectivity that subverts external definitions of her female self; as Joanne Frye argues, "Saying 'I am' is itself one of the most powerful expressions of a woman's capacity to resist cultural definitions" (64).

This change of plot in the Chicana *Bildungsroman,* from entrapment in a male-defined destiny in *Victuum* and *Trini* to a subjective affirmation of a self-defined female identity in *The House on Mango Street* and *The Last of the Menu Girls,* is accompanied by narrative strategies that accentuate the fragmented, nonlinear nature of female development. Each narrative is centered in the consciousness of a narrating "I," who, through her own subjective and nonchronological recollections, renders the essential periods and experiences that formed an important part of her *Bildungs* process. Here the narratives, unlike in the previous two novels, do not follow a linear process that leads the protagonist from adolescence to maturity and the seemingly inevitable marriage; rather, each narrative is composed of fragments of insights and experiences that in some way heighten the protagonist's consciousness about her own development as a woman within a particular socio-cultural context. This narrative strategy subverts the traditional form of the genre and underscores that the Chicana *Bildungsroman* must break out of that mold in order to reflect the fragmented nature of the Chicana developmental process.

This series of experiences, however, which heightens the protagonist's consciousness about her own development as a Chicana, only takes on coherence and meaning through the protagonist's own creative interpretation of her developmental process. The narrative "I" discovers a pattern of meaning, her *Bildung,* in the very act of creating her own story. The creativity of the budding Chicana writer forms an integral part of her *Bildungs* process. This interconnection between creativity and a self-defined female identity underscores Carolyn Heilbrun's argument that "women come to writing . . . simultaneously with self-creation" (1988, 117). In both novels the underlying quest for identity is thus portrayed as intimately connected with the concept of the discovery of self through the process of creation. The Chicana *Bildungsheld* must imagine herself into being. It is through an act of the imagination that she envisions her own self-realization as a Chicana writer. This interplay between self-development and the creative imagination turns each of these two novels into a *Künstlerroman,* as the creativity of the Chicana *Bildungsheld* is the catalyst for her own self-discovery. In the process of this creative self-discovery the Chicana narrator/protagonist/artist forges a new relationship between self and community.

It is significant that at the end of both *The House on Mango Street* and *The Last of the Menu Girls* each protagonist makes a symbolic return to the Chicano community. This reinforcement of community ties, an acknowledgement of the important role of the community in each *Bildungs* process, forms an integral part of each novel. In *The House on Mango Street,* Esperanza's development takes place in the midst of a community of women whose socio-economic entrapment becomes a catalyst for her own quest for a distinct destiny. It becomes clear that this community of women also imbues her creative endeavors with a meaningful purpose, when she in the end expresses a desire to use her writing as a means to liberate women from patriarchal oppression. The expressed purpose of the protagonist's symbolic return on the final pages of *The Last of the Menu Girls* is to dedicate her writing to the Chicano community and particularly to her mother's house. This creative dedication to the community is reflected not only thematically in the protagonist's exploration of her barrio in southern New Mexico; it is also reflected in the very language that narrator uses to express her recollections. Woven into her reminiscences are bilingual dialogues and phrases that capture the particularities of a border milieu. Phrases such as "Tamales de La Buena! Qué treat!" (188) and "For chanza me dieron ride, comadre" (175) are textual reflections of a bicultural community whose members move smoothly between two linguistic codes, thus capturing the cultural idiosyncrasies of a Mexican/American border context.

Bildung as Subversive Act

In both *The House on Mango Street* and *The Last of the Menu Girls,* the Chicana protagonist uses her creativity to claim her identity as a unique, self-defined woman. This self-definition emerges out of a conscious opposition to patriarchal norms and values. Through the act of narrating her own *Bildungs* story, the Chicana protagonist claims not only her individual subjectivity, but a subjectivity that is rooted in a shared socio-cultural context. The discovery of self through the process of creation is thus intimately connected to the discovery of an ethnic self, a Chicana identity that is based on a conscious recognition of her position as a woman within the Chicano community. In the process of critiquing, understanding, and celebrating her own personal history, the Chicana "I" reformulates the Chicano experience from a feminist perspective, forging in the process a new relationship between the Chicana, self, and the Chicano community.

CONCLUSION
TOWARD A DEFINITION OF THE CHICANA *BILDUNGSROMAN/ KÜNSTLERROMAN*

The way we imagine our lives is the way we are going to go on living our lives.
—JAMES HILLMAN

"The simple act of telling a woman's story from a woman's point of view is a revolutionary act," writes Carol Christ. "It has never been done before" (1980, 7). When it comes to the Chicana, who has been constricted simultaneously by Anglo as well as by Chicano stereotypes of her Chicana identity, her movement into the *Bildungsroman* genre in order to explore her own rites of passage as a Chicana is a doubly revolutionary act. In her exploration of the Chicana *Bildungs* process, the writer of each of the four Chicana *Bildungsromane* included in this study brings to literature distinct Chicana perspectives and experiences that transform, not only the traditional male-defined quest story, but the traditional female quest story as well.

White women writers have transformed the traditional *Bildungsroman* by including the question of gender as a determining factor in the process of self-development, but they have tended to focus exclusively upon patriarchal oppression of women and to ignore the influence ethnicity and class may have upon the female *Bildungs* process. Although patriarchal oppression is a central theme throughout these Chicana *Bildungsromane*, it is not the only form of oppression the Chicana *Bildungsheld* has to contend with. Chicana writers are conscious of the fact that "'one becomes a woman' in ways that are much more complex than in a simple opposition to men" (Alarcón, 1990, 360), and that questions of race and class are crucial components of the female developmental experience. This consciousness of difference, which goes far beyond mere gender consciousness, distinguishes the Chicana *Bildungsroman* from its Anglo counterpart. Building on their own historical circumstances, Chicana *Bildungsroman* writers expand the female quest story by exploring the crucial effects particular ethnic contexts and patterns of economic deprivation have on the female developmental process.

Each *Bildungsroman* of this study is situated within a distinct Chicano context: *Victuum* takes place within an old Hispanic community in California; *Trini* portrays the journey north from Mexico and into the United States; *The House on Mango Street* explores the urban barrio experience; and *The Last of the Menu Girls* is set in the border milieu of southern New Mexico. These different settings represent and affirm distinct historical backgrounds and socio-cultural circumstances that inform the Chicano experience in the United States. Intertwined with the cultural heritage that each of these settings represents is also a heritage of deprivation and oppression, which, in varying degrees, influences the Chicana's perception, not only of her own ethnic identity, but of that of her entire community. In claiming such heritage, the Chicana *Bildungsroman* shares common grounds with its Chicano counterpart. The Chicano/Chicana *Bildungsheld* is situated within a family tradition and a cultural context that, by its very existence, stands in opposition to a hegemonic culture. Much like the protagonists of Chicano *Bildungsromane* such as . . . *y no se lo tragó la tierra* by Tomás Rivera, *Bless Me Ultima* by Rudolfo Anaya, and *The Rain God* by Arturo Islas, the ethnic identity of the Chicana *Bildungsheld* is formed within a socio-cultural context in which oppression and resistance play major roles.

In the Chicana *Bildungsroman,* the ethnic experience is presented from a female perspective, a perspective through which such cultural heritage takes on distinct characteristics. Each novel illustrates to some degree Irene Campos Carr's observation that "Chicanas carry an additional burden of internal oppression by a cultural heritage that tends to be dominated by males and exaggerates male domination over women" (269). In both *Victuum* and *Trini,* the protagonist's *Bildungs* process is defined by a traditional patriarchal context, a process that leads each protagonist to accept a prescribed destiny of wife and mother; when the protagonists later awaken to the entrapment these roles present, they seek solace in an extra-social psychic or natural sphere beyond the Chicano community. It is only when the Chicana protagonist begins to narrate her *Bildungs* process from her own experiential perspective that we encounter a conscious exploration of ethnic heritage and patriarchal norms and values. In both *The House on Mango Street* and *The Last of the Menu Girls,* the ethnic experience is filtered through the consciousness of the Chicana protagonist who, through the act of narrating, enters into an active engagement with different aspects of her cultural heritage. It is this engagement that leads to an opposition to patriarchal norms and values while affirming other aspects of her ethnic identity. Narrating her own story, the Chicana protagonist explores the relationship between self and community, a process of creative self-formation that at the same time is her own redefinition of her Chicana identity.

A constant theme throughout these novels is the influence of economic circumstances and the consequent social stratification and marginalization of women's lives. In both *Victuum* and *Trini,* the protagonist's psychological dependency on men is aggravated by extreme poverty, creating a double dependency that precludes any quest for autonomy. *The House on Mango Street* explores to a great extent the link between poverty and female self-development. Esperanza is thus surrounded by women who have been brought up to believe that only a man can rescue them from economic oppression in the barrio, a notion that leads to a cycle of female dependency, confinement, and violence that the women are unable to break. Esperanza's desire to escape such confinement becomes the catalyst for her quest for selfhood. This novel, furthermore, explores the negative psychological impact poverty has on the protagonist's self-perception, an impact she is able to overcome only through her imaginative creation of a poetic space of her own.

Collectively, the Chicana *Bildungsromane* of this study portray an important development in Chicana consciousness. From *Victuum* and *Trini* to *The House on Mango Street* and *The Last of the Menu Girls,* four different Chicana *Bildungs* experiences are outlined that present an evolutionary movement from victimization to conscious self-affirmation. Valentina and Trini undergo a *Bildungs* process that leads directly to entrapment in prescribed roles and socio-cultural alienation. *The House on Mango Street* and *The Last of the Menu Girls* replace this traditional ending of the female quest story by presenting a different developmental process and alternative destinies for the Chicana protagonist. From Valentina's passive acceptance of her husband's prohibitions to Rocío's assertive self-definition, "Yes. I am a writer," the Chicana *Bildungsromane* articulate opposition to patriarchal domination as well as new concepts of Chicana identity. Through the liberating act of writing, the Chicana *Bildungsheld* of these two novels become conscious of their Chicana identity, and through their writing they affirm their bond to the Chicano community.

This development in Chicana consciousness, from victimization to creative self-affirmation of Chicana identity, is accompanied by narrative strategies that move away from the traditional linear, chronological convention of the genre. By disrupting this male-defined narrative paradigm, the narrator/protagonist/writer underscores that the Chicana needs a different fragmented and nonlinear form to re-create her own *Bildungs* experience. Significantly, it is when the Chicana protagonist claims narrative authority of her own *Bildungs* story that the story takes on a new form. Thus the Chicana writer, the *Künstler*, subverts the traditional *Bildungsroman* in both content and form, and through her own creative perspective, transforms her *Bildung* into a process of liberating self-creation.

With the Chicana *Bildungsroman*, a new figure has been introduced to the literary scene: the Chicana *Bildungsheld*. In the process Chicana writers have expanded the genre. Although the Chicana *Bildungsroman*, by its very nature, has certain features in common with both the traditional female *Bildungsroman* and the Chicano *Bildungsroman*, it expands the boundaries of both. In traditional female *Bildungsromane*, patriarchy is the main opponent of female self-definition. The Chicana self, however, is formed in opposition to multiple layers of oppression: the oppositional relationship between socio-cultural context and the female self is, when it comes to Chicana *Bildung*, intensified by questions of ethnicity and class. Because her social and cultural points of reference are multiple, she is unable to accept either Anglo-American or Chicano definitions of herself. As Norma Alarcón argues,

> An unquestioned Mexican and Chicano male culture
> represent a past that may lock her into some crippling
> traditional stereotypes, while the future has been
> represented within an Anglo-American feminist promise . . .
> a dream derived from what to a Chicana is an alien culture
> and rhetoric riddled with barriers to her attempt to
> articulate her sense of self. (1985, 87)

The Chicana *Bildungsroman* overcomes these barriers when the Chicana protagonist/writer claims the right to articulate her own experiences from her own perspective, to name and create her own image of herself. The self she creates is not one who strives for the autonomy and individuality which Anglo-American feminism has posited as a sine qua non of female development; rather, it is a self who is rooted in the ethnic experience, who defines herself in relation to family, community, and its traditions. Thus the search for self, which the *Bildungs* process presents, goes beyond a sovereign self to a communal self. She is, to use Alarcón's term, a "multiple-voiced subject" who has to forge a new identity among, and often in opposition to, a multiplicity of contending forces.

Articulating her sense of herself, Chicana writers have used the *Bildungsroman* to trace the development of complex and multidimensional Chicana *Bildungsheld*. In the process the Chicana writers subvert in content and form "the confining expectations of both narrative and life" (J. Frye, 83), that is, the traditional gender as well as genre limitations of the female quest story. Together the *Bildungsromane* of this study form a narrative of the Chicana self in the process of becoming, yet these are but the first chapters of a broader Chicana narrative of self.

NOTES

Introduction

1. German literary terminology makes a precise distinction between the *Bildungsroman* and its variants, the *Entwicklungsroman* and the *Erziehungsroman:* the *Entwicklungsroman,* the novel of development, is the most general term and suggests any growth or development of the protagonist without any indication of a particular goal; in contrast, the *Bildungsroman* depicts the growth toward a particular *Bildungsideal,* the development of a full and harmonious personality resulting from social and cultural interaction; the *Erziehungsroman* is a distinctly pedagogical and didactic novel giving particular attention to the influences of educational institutions. In English, however, these terms have become synonymous and are largely used interchangeably without the original German distinction. As G. B. Tennyson points out in his discussion of these terms, "a good deal of the concept of the *Entwicklungsroman,* the comprehensive 'novel of development' idea, seems to have come across the channel with the word *Bildungsroman* and to have strongly colored the English use of the term. . . . *Bildungsroman* in English has come to mean by itself what the *Bildungsroman,* the *Entwicklungsroman,* and the *Erziehungsroman* mean separately in German" (138).

2. Among the general studies on the tradition and development of the *Bildungsroman* are *The German Tradition of Self-Cultivation: Bildung from Humbolt to Thomas Mann* (1975) by Walter Horace Bruford, "Entwicklungs- und Bildungsroman: Ein Forschungsbericht" (1968) in two parts by Lothar Köhn, *The German Bildungsroman from Wieland to Hesse* (1978) by Martin Swales, *Bildung and Verbildung in the Prose Works of Otto Julius Bierbaum* (1974) by Roy L. Ackerman, *The Apprenticeship Novel* (1984) by Randolph P. Shaffner, "The Transformation of *Bildung* from an Image to an Ideal" by Susan L. Cocalis, "The 'Bildungsroman' in Germany, England, and France" by François Jost, "Kafka's Hapless Pilgrims and Grass's Scurrilous Dwarf: Notes on Representative Figures in the Anti-Bildungsroman" and "The Picaro's Journey to the Confessional: The

Changing Image of the Hero in the German Bildungsroman" by David H. Miles, "'Wilhelm Meisters Lehrjahre,' ein Bildungsroman?" by Kurt May, and "The *Bildungsroman* and Its Significance in the History of Realism" by M. M. Bakhtin. Studies focusing exclusively on British examples of the genre are Susan Howe's *Wilhelm Meister and His English Kinsmen* (1930), *Der englishe Bildungsroman bis in der Zeit des ersten Weltkrieges* (1951) by Hans Wagner, *Season of Youth: The Bildungsroman from Dickens to Golding* (1974) by Jerome Hamilton Buckley, and "The Bildungsroman in Nineteenth-Century English Literature" by G. B. Tennyson. Included in the American *Bildungsroman* tradition are Robert S. Bickham's dissertation *The Origins and Importance of the Initiation Story in the Twentieth-Century British and American Fiction* (1961), "Postmodern Bildungsromane: The Drama of Recent Autobiography" by Paul Christensen, "An Old Form Revitalized: Philip Roth's *Ghost Writer* and the *Bildungsroman*" by W. Clar Handley, "The *Bildungsroman*, American Style" by C. Hugh Holman, and "Der deutsche Bildungsroman in Amerika" by Volkmar Sander.

3. For critical discussions on the Chicano *Bildungsroman* and *Künstlerroman*, see "*Pocho:* Bildungsroman of a Chicano" by Carl R. Shirley, "Portraits of the Chicano Artist as a Young Man. The Making of the 'Author' in Three Chicano Novels" by Juan Bruce-Novoa, and "Growing Up Chicano: Tomás Rivera and Sandra Cisneros" by Erlinda Gonzales-Berry and Tey Diana Rebolledo.

4. Noted examples typifying the male-oriented *Bildungsroman* are, in England, *David Copperfield* and *Great Expectations* by Charles Dickens, *The Way of All Flesh* by Samuel Butler, *Sons and Lovers* by D. H. Lawrence, *Of Human Bondage* by Somerset Maugham, *A Portrait of the Artist as a Young Man* by James Joyce, and in the United States novels such as *Look Homeward, Angel* by Thomas Wolfe, *Arrowsmith* by Sinclair Lewis, *Go Down, Moses* by William Faulkner, *Catcher in the Rye* by J. D. Salinger, *The Adventures of Augie March* by Saul Bellow, *Winesburg, Ohio* by Sherwood Anderson, *The Book of Daniel* by E. L. Doctorow, *Go Tell It on the Mountain* by James Baldwin, *Pocho* by José Antonio Villarreal, ... *y no se lo tragó la tierra* by Tomás Rivera, and many others. One should not assume that the African-American and the Chicano *Bildungsroman* do not differ from the Anglo *Bildungsroman,* but it is not within the scope of this study to assess these differences.

5. Examples of the female *Bildungsroman* are *The Awakening* by Kate Chopin, *My Antonia* by Willa Cather, *The Heart Is a Lonely Hunter* and *The Member of the Wedding* by Carson McCullers, *The Bell Jar* by Sylvia Plath, *Daughter of Earth* by Agnes Smedley, *Bread Givers* by

Anzia Yezierska, *The Woman Warrior* by Maxine Hong Kingston, *Their Eyes Were Watching God* by Zora Neal Hurston, *Brown Girl, Brownstones* by Paule Marshall, *Daddy Was a Number Runner* by Louise Meriwether, *The Bluest Eye* by Toni Morrison, *The Jailing of Cecelia Capture* by Janet Campbell Hale, and *The Woman Who Owned the Shadows* by Paula Gunn Allen, among many others.

6. Among relevant articles on the female *Bildungsroman* are "Alther, Atwood, Ballantyne, and Gray: Secular Salvation in the Contemporary Feminist Bildungsroman," "*Bildung* in Ethnic Women Writers," and "New Directions in the Contemporary Bildungsroman: Lisa Alther's *Kinflicks*" by Bonnie Hoover Braendlin; "The Female Novel of Development and the Myth of Psyche" by Mary Ann Ferguson; "The Female Initiation Theme in American Fiction" by Elaine Ginsberg; "The Brother, the Twin: Women Novelists and Male-Female Double *Bildungsroman*" by Charlotte Goodman; "The Novel of Formation as Genre: Between Great Expectations and Lost Illusions" and "Spiritual *Bildung:* The Beautiful Soul as Paradigm" by Marianne Hirsch; "The Feminine Bildungsroman: Education Through Marriage" by Elaine Hoffman Baruch; "The Afro-American and the Afro-Caribbean Female *Bildungsroman*" by Geta LeSeur; "Race, Sex and Self: Aspects of *Bildung* in Select Novels by Black American Women Novelists" by Sondra O'Neale; "The Novel of Awakening" by Susan J. Rosowski; "The Limits of Domesticity: The Female *Bildungsroman* in America, 1820–1870" by Beverly R. Voloshin; "Plath's *The Bell Jar* as Female *Bildungsroman*" by Linda W. Wagner; and essays in *The Voyage In: Fictions of Female Development* (1981) edited by Elizabeth Abel, Marianne Hirsch, and Elizabeth Langland.

7. Among the studies on the female *Bildungsroman* only three articles discuss racial or ethnic variations of the developmental theme: "The Afro-American and the Afro-Caribbean Female *Bildungsroman*" by Geta LeSeur, "Race, Sex and Self: Aspects of *Bildung* in Select Novels by Black American Women Novelists" by Sondra O'Neale, and "*Bildung* in Ethnic Women Writers" by Bonnie Hoover Braendlin; the latter is the only article to include a Chicana novel in its analysis of the genre. An article devoted exclusively to the Chicano/Chicana *Bildungsroman* is "Growing Up Chicano: Tomás Rivera and Sandra Cisneros" by Erlinda Gonzales-Berry and Tey Diana Rebolledo.

Chapter 1

1. The first Chicana novel to be published is *Come Down from the Mound* (1975) by Berta Ornelas; for further publication informa-

tion, see "Isabella Ríos and the Chicano Psychic Novel" and "Chicana Novelists in the Process of Creating Fictive Voices" by Francisco A. Lomelí.

2. For a discussion on the influence of the oral tradition in Chicano literature, see "Mexican American Literature: A Historical Perspective" by Luis Leal, "Chicano Literature: An Overview" by Luis Leal and Pepe Barrón, and "The Evolution of Chicano Literature" by Raymund A. Paredes.

3. For further discussion and information on these early Hispanic women writers see "Tradition and Mythology: Signatures of Landscape in Chicana Literature" and "Hispanic Woman Writers of the Southwest: Tradition and Innovation" by Tey Diana Rebolledo, "Chicana Novelists in the Process of Creating Fictive Voices" by Francisco A. Lomelí, and "Cultural Ambivalence in Early Chicana Literature" by Gloria Velásquez Treviño.

4. The publication history of *Victuum* exemplifies the difficulties Chicanas and other ethnic women writers have when it comes to having their work published; *Victuum* was published through the author's own efforts, funded partly by herself, partly by friends and relatives. Information on the particular circumstances surrounding the creation and publication of *Victuum,* including biographical information on the author, can be found in "Isabella Ríos and the Chicano Psychic Novel," which includes an interview with the author, and "Chicana Novelists in the Process of Creating Fictive Voices" by Francisco A. Lomelí, and "Isabella Ríos" by Annie O. Eysturoy.

Chapter 2

1. For further elaboration on the primary meaning of the term *Bildung* and its relation to the terms *Bild* and *imago,* see François Jost, "The 'Bildungsroman' in Germany, England, and France," 135–36; Susan L. Cocalis, "The Transformation of *Bildung* From an Image to an Ideal"; and Bonnie Hoover Braendlin, *Bildung and the Role of Women in the Edwardian Bildungsroman: Maugham, Bennett, and Wells,* 28–29.

2. Novels such as *Pocho* (1959) by José Antonio Villarreal and *Chicano* (1970) take their point of departure in Mexico, trace the migration north into the United States and explore the consequent social and economic changes caused by migration and exploitation in the United States. These novels are marred by female stereotypes. In *Pocho,* Consuelo is portrayed as causing the disintegration of the family and traditions by her irresponsible desire for American-style female independence. The female protagonist in *Chicano,* Mariana,

is punished with death for her sexual transgressions with an Anglo; her name identifies her with La Malinche, also known as Malintzín or Marina, who according to Mexican myth was the supposed betrayer of her people.

3. Naming and its opposite, imposed silence and the consequent loss of identity, is a recurrent motif in contemporary women's literature. An outstanding example is Maxine Hong Kingston's haunting tale "No Name Woman," which forms part of *The Woman Warrior.* For critical discussions on the act of naming, see, for example, *Diving Deep and Surfacing: Women Writers on Spiritual Quest* by Carol P. Christ, *Beyond God the Father* by Mary Daly, and *On Lies, Secrets, and Silence* by Adrienne Rich.

4. For a feminist revision of the Malinche myth, see for example "Chicana's Feminist Literature: A Re-Vision Through Malintzin/or Malintzin: Putting Flesh Back on the Object" by Norma Alarcón and "La Malinche, Feminist Prototype" by Cordelia Candelaria.

Chapter 3

1. There is a wide discrepancy among critics about how to define the narrative structure, the genre, of *The House on Mango Street*. I have chosen to define its narrative structure as interrelated stories that in their entirety form a novel, a *Bildungsroman*. For a discussion on the question of genre in *The House on Mango Street* see "Género e ideología en el libro de Sandra Cisneros: *The House on Mango Street*" by Pedro Gutiérrez-Revuelta.

GLOSSARY

Bildungsroman (pl.-e): novel of development, coming of age novel, apprenticeship novel.

Bildung: formation, education, development.

Bildungs- : compound -s, when used with another noun.

Bildungsheld: the hero of the Bildungsroman.

Bildungsideal: the specific ideal formation which the traditional German Bildungsroman hero was supposed to obtain.

Künstlerroman (pl. -e): the novel that deals with the development of the artist or writer.

SOURCES CITED

Primary Literature

Chávez, Denise. *The Last of the Menu Girls.* Houston, Tex.: Arte Público Press, 1986.

Cisneros, Sandra. *The House on Mango Street.* Houston, Tex.: Arte Público Press, 1985.

Portillo Trambley, Estela. *Trini.* Binghamton, N.Y.: Bilingual Press/ Editorial Bilingüe, 1986.

Ríos, Isabella. *Victuum.* Ventura, Calif.: Diana-Etna, 1976.

Secondary Literature

General

Abel, Elizabeth. "(E)merging Identities: The Dynamics of Female Friendship in Contemporary Fiction by Women." *Signs* 6, no. 3 (1981): 413–44.

———, Marianne Hirsch, and Elizabeth Langland, eds. "Introduction." *The Voyage In: Fictions of Female Development,* 3–29. Hanover & London: University Press of New England, 1983.

Ackerman, Roy L. *Bildung und Verbildung in the Prose Works of Otto Julius Bierbaum.* Bern, Switzerland: Herbert Lang, 1974.

Awkward, Michael. "Race, Gender, and the Politics of Reading." *Black American Literature Forum* 22, no.1 (Spring 1988): 5–27.

Bachelard, Gaston. *The Poetics of Space.* Boston: Beacon Press, 1994.

Bakerman, Jane S. "Failures of Love: Female Initiation in the Novels of Toni Morrison." *American Literature* 52, no.4 (Jan. 1981): 541–63.

Bakhtin, M. M. *The Dialogic Imagination.* Austin: University of Texas Press, 1981.

———. "The *Bildungsroman* and Its Significance in the History of Realism." *Speech Genres and Other Late Essays,* 10–59. Austin: University of Texas Press, 1986.

Bannan, Helen M. "Spider Woman's Web: Mothers and Daughters in Southwestern Native American Literature." In *The Lost Tradition: Mothers and Daughters in Fiction,* edited by Cathy N. Davidson and E. M. Broner, 168–79. New York: Frederick Ungar, 1980.

Beauvoir, Simone de. *The Second Sex.* New York: Vintage Books, 1974.

Beebe, Maurice. *Ivory Towers and Sacred Founts: The Artist as Hero in Fiction from Goethe to Joyce.* New York: New York University Press, 1964.

Belsey, Catherine. "Constructing the Subject: Deconstructing the Text." In *Feminist Criticism and Social Change,* edited by G. Newton and D. Rosenfelt, 45–64. New York: Methuen, 1985.

Benjamin, Walter. *Illuminations.* N.p.: Fontana, 1973.

Bennett, Paula. *My Life a Loaded Gun: Female Creativity and Feminist Poetics.* Boston: Beacon Press, 1986.

Benstock, Shari, ed. *The Private Self: Theory and Practice of Women's Autobiographical Writings.* Chapel Hill: University of North Carolina Press, 1988.

Bickham, Robert S. "The Origins and Importance of the Initiation Story in the Twentieth Century British and American Fiction." Ph.D. diss., University of New Mexico, 1961.

Bloom, Lynn Z. "Heritages: Dimensions of Mother-Daughter Relationships in Women's Autobiographies." In *The Lost Tradition: Mothers and Daughters in Fiction,* edited by Cathy N. Davidson and E. M. Broner, 291–303. New York: Frederick Ungar, 1980.

Boelen, Bernard J. *Personal Maturity: The Existential Dimension.* New York: The Seabury Press, 1978.

Boelhower, William. *Through a Glass Darkly: Ethnic Semiosis in American Literature.* New York: Oxford University Press, 1987.

Booth, Wayne C. "Freedom of Interpretation: Bakhtin and the Challenge of Feminist Criticism." *Critical Inquiry* 9, no.1 (Sept. 1982): 45–76.

Braendlin, Bonnie Hoover. "*Bildung* and the Role of Women in the Edwardian Bildungsroman: Maugham, Bennett, and Wells." Ph.D diss., Florida State University, 1978.

————. "Alther, Atwood, Ballantyne, and Gray: Secular Salvation in the Contemporary Feminist Bildungsroman." *Frontiers* 4, no.1 (1979): 18–22.

————. "New Directions in the Contemporary Bildungsroman: Lisa Alther's *Kinflicks*." In *Gender and Literary Voice*, edited by Janet Todd, 169–71. New York: Holmes and Meier, 1980.

————. "*Bildung* in Ethnic Women Writers." *Denver Quarterly* 17, no.4 (Winter 1983): 75–87.

Brown, Cheryl L., and Karen Olson, eds. *Feminist Criticism: Essays on Theory, Poetry and Prose*. Metuchen, N.J.: Scarecrow Press, 1978.

Brownstein, Rachel M. *Becoming a Heroine: Reading about Women in Novels*. New York: Penguin Books, 1982.

Bruford, Walter Horace. *The German Tradition of Self-Cultivation: Bildung from Humbolt to Thomas Mann*. Cambridge: Cambridge University Press, 1975.

Buckley, Jerome Hamilton. *Season of Youth: The Bildungsroman from Dickens to Golding*. Cambridge, Mass.: Harvard University Press, 1974.

Burke, Kenneth. "Literature as Equipment for Living." In *The Philosophy of Literary Form*, 253–62. Baton Rouge: Louisiana State University Press, 1967.

Calisher, Hortense. "No Important Women Writer." In *Women's Liberation and Literature*, edited by Elaine Showalter, 223–30. New York: Harcourt Brace Jovanovich, 1971.

Campbell, Joseph. *The Hero With a Thousand Faces*. N.J.: Princeton University Press, 1973.

Campbell, Josie P. "The Woman as Hero in Margaret Atwood's *Surfacing*." *Mosaic* 11, no.3 (Spring 1978): 17–28.

Carby, Hazel V. "The Canon: Civil War and Reconstruction." *Michigan Quarterly Review* (Spring 1989): 35–43.

Chowdorow, Nancy. "Family Structure and Feminine Personality." In *Woman, Culture, and Society*, edited by Michelle Zimbalist Rosaldo and Louise Lamphere, 43–66. Stanford: Stanford University Press, 1974.

————. "Feminism and Difference." *Socialist Review* 46 (July– Aug. 1979): 51–69.

Christ, Carol P. "Margaret Atwood: The Surfacing of Women's Spiritual Quest and Vision. *Signs* 2, no.2 (1976): 316–30.

————. "Imaginative Constraint, Feminine Duty, and the Form of Charlotte Brontë's Fiction." *Women's Studies* 6, no.3 (1979): 287–96.

————. *Diving Deep and Surfacing: Women Writers on Spiritual Quest.* Boston: Beacon Press, 1980.

Christensen, Paul. "Postmodern Bildungsromans: The Drama of Recent Autobiography." *Sagetrieb* 5, no.1 (Spring 1986): 29–40.

Christian, Barbara. "Trajectories of Self-Definition: Placing Contemporary Afro-American Women's Fiction." In *Conjuring: Black Women, Fiction, and Literary Tradition,* edited by Marjorie Pryse and Hortense J. Spillers, 233–48. Bloomington: Indiana University Press, 1985.

————. "The Race for Theory." *Feminist Studies* 14, no.1 (Spring 1988): 67–79.

Cixous, Hélène. "Sorties." In *New French Feminism: An Anthology,* edited by Elaine Marks and Isabelle de Courtivron, 90–98. New York: Schocken Books, 1980.

————. "The Laugh of the Medusa." In *New French Feminism: An Anthology,* edited by Elaine Marks and Isabelle de Courtivron, New York: Schocken Books, 1980.

————. "Castration or Decapitation?" *Signs* 7, no.1 (Autumn 1981): 41–55

Cocalis, Susan L. "The Transformation of *Bildung* from an Image to an Ideal." *Monatschefte* 70, no.4 (1978): 339–414.

Coyle, William. *The Young Man in American Literature.* New York: Odyssey Press, 1969.

Crites, Stephen. "The Narrative Quality of Experience." *Journal of the American Academy of Religion* 39, no.3 (Sept. 1971): 291–311.

Crowder, Diane Griffin. "Amazons and Mothers: Monique Wittig, Hélène Cixous and Theories of Women's Writing." *Contemporary Literature* 24, no.2 (1983): 117–44.

Daly, Mary. *Beyond God the Father: Toward a Philosophy of Women's Liberation.* Boston: Beacon Press, 1973.

Davidson, Cathy N., and E. M. Broner, eds. *The Lost Tradition: Mothers and Daughters in Fiction.* New York: Frederick Unger, 1980.

Dearborn, Mary V. *Pocahontas's Daughters: Gender and Ethnicity in American Culture.* New York: Oxford University Press, 1986.

Dellas, Marie, and Eugene L. Gaier. "The Self and Adolescent Identity in Women: Options and Implications." *Adolescence* 10, no.39 (Fall 1975): 399–407.

Diltey, W. *Das Erlebnis und die Dichtung: Lessing, Goethe, Novalis, Hölderlin.* Göttingen: Vandenhoeck & Ruprecht, 1965.

Eagleton, Terry. "Text, Ideology, Realism." In *Literature and Society,* edited by Edward W. Said, 149–73. Baltimore & London: Johns Hopkins University Press, 1980.

Edwards, Lee R. "The Labors of Psyche: Towards a Theory of Female

Heroism." *Critical Inquiry* 6, no.1 (Autumn 1979): 33–49.

Eichner, Hans. "The Eternal Feminine: An Aspect of Goethe's Ethics." In Johann Wolfgang von Goethe. *Faust*, edited by Cyrus Hamlin. New York: Norton Critical Edition, 1976.

Ellman, Mary. "Phallic Criticism." In *Women's Liberation and Literature*, edited by Elaine Showalter, 213–22. New York: Harcourt Brace Jovanovich, 1971.

Erikson, Erik H. "Inner and Outer Space: Reflections on Womanhood." *Daedalus* 93 (1964): 582–606.

Felman, Shoshana. "Women and Madness: The Critical Phallacy." *Diacritics* 5, no.4 (Winter 1975): 2–10.

Ferguson, Mary Anne. "The Female Novel of Development and the Myth of the Psyche." *Denver Quarterly* 17, no.4 (Winter 1983): 58–74.

Fisher, Michael. "The Imagination as a Sanction of Value: Northrop Frye and the Usefulness of Literature." In *Does Deconstruction Make Any Difference?* 14–31. Bloomington: Indiana University Press, 1985.

Fluck, Winifried. "Literature as Symbolic Action." *Americastudies* 28, no.3 (1984): 361–71.

Freire, Paolo. *The Pedagogy of the Oppressed.* New York: Continuum, 1984.

Freud, Sigmund. *Three Essays on the Theory of Sexuality.* New York: Basic Books, 1962.

Friday, Nancy. *My Mother/My Self: The Daughter's Search for Identity.* New York: Delacorte Press, 1977.

Friedan, Sandra. *Autobiography: Self Into Form.* Vol. 2, *Forschungen zur Literatur- und Kulturgeschichte.* Frankfurt am Main: Verlag Peter Lang, 1983.

Frye, Joanne S. *Living Stories, Telling Lives: Women and the Novel in Contemporary Experience.* Ann Arbor: The University of Michigan Press, 1986.

Frye, Northrop. *Fables of Identity: Studies in Poetic Mythology.* New York: Harcourt, Brace & World, 1963.

———. *Anatomy of Criticism: Four Essays.* Princeton, N.J.: Princeton University Press, 1973.

Fuderer, Laura Sue. *The Female Bildungsroman in English: An Annotated Bibliography of Criticism.* New York: The Modern Language Association of America, 1990.

Gardiner, Judith Kegan. "The Heroine as Her Author's Daughter." In *Feminist Criticism: Essays on Theory, Poetry and Prose,* edited by Cheryl L. Brown and Karen Olson, 244–53. Metuchen, N.J.: Scarecrow Press, 1978.

————. "On Female Identity and Writing by Women." *Critical Inquiry* 8, no.2 (1981): 347–61.

Gates, Henry Louis Jr., ed. *"Race,"Writing, and Difference.* Chicago & London: University of Chicago Press, 1986.

Gilbert, Sandra M., and Susan Gubar. *The Madwoman in the Attic: The Woman Writer and the Nineteenth-Century Literary Imagination.* New Haven, Conn.: Yale University Press, 1979.

Gilligan, Carol. *In a DifferentVoice: Psychological Theory andWomen's Development.* Cambridge, Mass.: Harvard University Press, 1982.

Ginsberg, Elaine. "The Female Initiation Theme in American Fiction." *Studies in American Fiction* 3, no.1 (Spring 1975): 27–37.

Goldberg, Gerald Jay. "The Artist-Novel in Transition." *English Fiction in Transition* 4, no.3 (1961): 12–27.

Goodman, Charlotte. "The Brother, the Twin: Women Novelists and Male-Female Double *Bildungsroman.*" *Novel* 17, no.1 (Fall 1983): 28–43.

Gubar, Susan. "'The Blank Page' and the Issues of Female Creativity." *Critical Inquiry* 8, no.2 (1981): 243–63.

————. "The Birth of the Artist as Heroine: (Re)production, the *Künstlerroman* Tradition, and the Fiction of Katherine Mansfield." In *The Representation of Women in Fiction,* edited by Carolyn G. Heilbrun and Margaret R. Higonnet, 15–59. Baltimore & London: Johns Hopkins University Press, 1981.

Hegel, G. W. F. *Vorlesungen über die Ästhetik.* Edited by F. Bassenge. Berlin, 1955.

Heilbrun, Carolyn G. *Reinventing Womanhood.* New York: W. W. Norton, 1979.

————. *Writing a Woman's Life.* New York: Ballantine Books, 1988.

———— and Margaret R. Higonnet, eds. *The Representation ofWomen in Fiction.* New Series 7. *Selected Papers from the English Institute.* Baltimore & London: Johns Hopkins University Press, 1981.

———— and Catharine R. Stimpson. "Theories of Feminist Criticism: A Dialogue." In *Feminist Literary Criticism,* edited by Josephine Donovan. Lexington, Ken.: University Press of Kentucky, 1975.

Heller, Dana A. *The Feminization of Quest-Romance: Radical Departures.* Austin: University of Texas Press, 1990.

Hendley, W. Clark. "An Old Form Revitalized: Philip Roth's *Ghost Writer* and the *Bildungsroman.*" *Studies in the Novel* 16, no.1 (Spring 1984): 87–100.

Hillman, James. *The Myth ofAnalysis.* NewYork: Harper & Row, 1978.

————. *Healing Fiction.* New York: Station Hill, 1983.

Hirsch, Marianne. "The Novel of Formation as Genre: Between Great Expectations and Lost Illusions." *Genre* 12, no.3 (Fall 1979): 293–311.

———. "Spiritual *Bildung*: The Beautiful Soul as Paradigm." In *The Voyage In: Fictions of Female Development*, edited by Elizabeth Abel, Marianne Hirsch, and Elizabeth Langland, 23–47. Hanover & London: University Press of New England. 1983.

Hoffman, Leonore, and Margo Culley, eds. *Women's Personal Narratives: Essays in Criticism and Pedagogy*. New York: The Modern Language Association of America, 1985.

Hoffman Baruch, Elaine. "The Feminine Bildungsroman: Education Through Marriage." *The Massachusetts Review* (Summer 1981): 335– 57.

Holland, Norman N. "Unity Identity Text Self." *PMLA* 90, no.5 (1975): 813–22.

Holman, C. Hugh. "The *Bildungsroman*, American Style." In *Windows on the World: Essays on American Social Fiction*, 168–97. Knoxville: University of Tennessee Press, 1979.

Hooks, Bell. *Feminist Theory: From Margin to Center*. Boston, Mass.: South End Press, 1987.

Howe, Susanne. *Wilhelm Meister and his English Kinsmen*. Columbia University Studies in English and Comparative Lit., no. 97. New York: Columbia University Press, 1930.

Huf, Linda. *A Portrait of the Artist as a Young Woman: The Writer as Heroine in American Literature*. New York: Frederick Ungar, 1983.

Hutcheon, Linda. *Narcissistic Narrative, The Metafictional Paradox*. New York & London: Methuen, 1984.

Jacobus, Mary. "Reading Woman (Reading)." In *Reading Woman: Essays in Feminist Criticism*, 3–24. New York: Columbia, 1980.

Jameson, Fredric. "The Symbolic Inference: or, Kenneth Burke and Ideological Analysis." *Critical Inquiry* 4 (1978): 507–23.

———. *The Political Unconscious: Narrative as a Socially Symbolic Act*. Ithaca, N.Y.: Cornell University Press, 1981.

Jehlen, Myra. "Archimedes and the Paradox of Feminist Criticism." *Signs* 6, no.4 (1981): 575–601.

Johnson, Thomas, ed. *The Poems of Emily Dickinson*. Cambridge: Harvard University Press, 1955.

Jones, Ann Rosalind. "Writing the Body: Toward an Understanding of l'écriture féminine." In *Feminist Criticism and Social Change*, edited by G. Newton, and D. Rosenfelt, 86–101. New York: Methuen, 1985.

Jost, François. "The 'Bildungsroman' in Germany, England, and France." *Introduction to Comparative Literature*, 134–60. Indianapolis & New York: Pegasus, 1974.

Kelly, R. Gordon. "Literature and the Historian." *American Quarterly* 26, no.2 (May 1974): 141–59.

Killoh, Ellen Peck. "The Woman Writer and the Element of Destruction." *College English* 34 (1972): 31–38.

Köhn, Lothar. "Entwicklungs- und Bildungsroman: Ein Forschungsbericht." (Erster Teil) *Deutsche Vierteljahrsschrift für Literaturwissenschaft und Geistesgeschichte* Jahrgang 42, Heft 3 (1968): 427–73.

————. "Entwicklungs- und Bildungsroman: Ein Forschungsbericht." (Zweiter Teil) *Deutsche Vierteljahrsschrift für Literaturwissenschaft und Geistesgeschichte* Jahrgang 42, Heft 4 (1968): 590–632.

Kolodny, Annette. "Some Notes on Defining a 'Feminist Literary Criticism.'" *Critical Inquiry* 2 (Autumn 1975): 75–92.

Kumar, Shiv. "Dorothy Richardson and the Dilemma of 'Being Versus Becoming.'" *Modern Language Notes* 74 (June 1959): 494–501.

Labovitz, Esther Kleinbord. *The Myth of the Heroine: The Female Bildungsroman in the Twentieth Century*. Vol 4, American University Studies Series 19. New York: Peter Lang, 1986.

Lacan, Jacques. *Écrits*. New York: W. W. Norton, 1977.

Laing, R. D. *The Politics of Experience*. New York: Ballantine Books, 1967.

Langland, Elizabeth. "Female Stories of Experience: Alcott's *Little Women* in Light of *Work*." In *The Voyage In: Fictions of Female Development*, edited by Marianne Hirsch and Elizabeth Langland, 112–27. Hanover & London: University Press of New England, 1983.

Lazzaro-Weis, Carol. "The Female *Bildungsroman*: Calling It Into Question." *NWSA Journal* 2, no.1 (Winter 1990): 16–34.

Lemon, Lee T. "Doris Lessing: From Fragmentation to Wholeness." *Portraits of the Artist in Contemporary Fiction*. Lincoln & London: University of Nebraska Press. 1985.

Lentricchia, Frank. *Criticism and Social Change*. Chicago: University of Chicago Press, 1983.

LeSeur, Geta. "The Afro-American and the Afro-Caribbean Female *Bildungsroman*." *The Black Scholar* 17, no.2 (March/April 1986): 26–33.

Levin, Harry. "Toward a Sociology of the Novel." In *Refractions*,

239–49. Oxford: Oxford University Press, 1966.

Lewis, R. W. B. *The American Adam*. Chicago & London: University of Chicago Press, 1955.

———. *The Picaresque Saint*. Chicago & London: University of Chicago Press, 1960.

Lionnet, Françoise. *Autobiographical Voices: Race, Gender, Self-Portraiture*. Ithaca & London: Cornell University Press, 1989.

Lorde, Audre. "Age, Race, Class, and Sex: Women Redefining Differences." In *Sister Outsider*, 114–23. Trumansburg, N.Y.: The Crossing Press, 1984.

Lukács, George. *Realism in Our Time*. New York: Harper & Row, 1964.

———. *The Theory of the Novel*. Cambridge: The MIT Press, 1971.

McCarty, Mari. "Possessing Female Space: 'The Tender Shoot.'" *Women's Studies* 8 (1981): 367–74.

McDowell, Deborah E. "New Directions for Black Feminist Criticism." In *The New Feminist Criticism: Essays on Women Literature Theory*, edited by Elaine Showalter, 186–99. New York: Pantheon Books, 1985.

Maglin, Nan Bauer. "'Don't Never Forget the Bridge That You Crossed Over On': The Literature of Matrilineage." In *The Lost Tradition: Mothers and Daughters in Fiction*, 257–67. New York: Frederick Ungar, 1980.

May, Kurt. "'Wilhelm Meisters Lehrjahre,' ein Bildungsroman?" *Deutsche Vierteljahrsschrift für Literaturwissenschaft und Geistesgeschichte* Jahrgang 31, Heft 1 (1957): 1–37.

Memmi, Albert. *The Colonizer and the Colonized*. New York: Orion Press, 1965.

Miles, David H. "Kafka's Hapless Pilgrims and Grass's Scurrilous Dwarf: Notes on Representative Figures in the Anti-Bildungsroman." *Monatshefte* 65, no.4 (Winter 1973): 341–50.

———. "The Picaro's Journey to the Confessional: The Changing Image of the Hero in the German Bildungsroman." *PMLA* 89, no.5 (1974): 980–92.

Morgan, Ellen. "Humanbecoming: Form and Focus in the Neo-Feminist Novel." In *Feminist Criticism: Essays of Theory, Poetry and Prose*, edited by Cheryl L. Brown and Karen Olson, 272–78. Metuchen, N.J.: Scarecrow Press, 1978.

Morrison, Toni. "Unspeakable Things Unspoken: The Afro-American Presence in American Literature." *Michigan Quarterly Review* (Spring 1989): 1–34.

Neuman, Erich. *Art and the Creative Unconscious*. Princeton: Princeton University Press, 1959.

Newton, Judith, and Deborah Rosenfelt. "Introduction: Toward a

Materialist-Feminist Criticism." In *Feminist Criticism and Social Change,* edited by Judith Newton and Deborah Rosenfelt, 15–39. New York & London: Methuen, 1985.

Olney, James. *Metaphors of Self: The Meaning of Autobiography.* Princeton: Princeton University Press, 1972.

Olsen, Tillie. *Silences.* New York: Dell, 1978.

O'Neale, Sondra. "Race, Sex and Self: Aspects of *Bildung* in Select Novels by Black American Women Novelists." *Melus* 9, no.4 (Winter 1982): 25–37.

Ortner, Sherry. "Is Female to Male as Nature Is to Culture?" In *Woman, Culture, and Society,* edited by Michelle Zimbalist Rosaldo and Louise Lamphere, 67–91. Palo Alto: Stanford University Press, 1974.

Ostriker, Alicia. "The Thieves of Language: Women Poets and Revisionist Mythmaking." *Signs* 8, no.11 (Autumn 1982): 68–90.

———. "Divided Selves: The Quest for Identity." In *Stealing the Language,* 59–90. Boston: Beacon Press, 1985.

Pearson, Carol, and Katherine Pope. *The Female Hero in American and British Literature.* New York: R. R. Bowker, 1981.

Pérez Firmat, Gustavo. "The Novel as Genre." *Genre* 12, no.3 (Fall 1979): 269–92.

Peterson, Carla L. "The Heroine as Reader in the Nineteenth-Century Novel: Emma Bovary and Maggie Tulliver." *Comparative Literature Studies* 17, no.2 (June 1980): 168–83.

Pratt, Annis. "The New Feminist Criticism." *College English* 32 (May 1971): 872–78.

———. "Archetypal Approaches to the New Feminist Criticism." *Bucknell Review* 21, no.1 (Spring 1973): 3–14.

———. *Archetypal Patterns to Women's Fiction.* Bloomington: Indiana University Press, 1981.

———. "Spinning Among Fields: Jung, Frye, Lévi-Strauss and Feminist Archetypal Theory." In *Feminist Archetypal Theory,* edited by Estella Lauter and Carol S. Rapprecht, 93–134. Knoxville: University of Tennessee Press, 1985.

Rabine, Leslie. "Problems of Textuality, History, and Ideology." In *Reading the Romantic Heroine: Text, History, Ideology,* 1–19. Ann Arbor: University of Michigan, 1985.

Rich, Adrienne. "When We Dead Awaken: Writing as Re-Vision." In *On Lies, Secrets, and Silence,* 33–49. New York: W. W. Norton, 1979.

Robinson, Lillian S. "Treason Our Text: Feminist Challenges to the Literary Canon." In *The New Feminist Criticism: Essays on Women, Literature, and Theory,* edited by Elaine Showalter,

105–21. New York: Pantheon Books, 1985.

Roller, Judi M. *The Politics of the Feminist Novel.* New York: Greenwood Press, 1986.

Ronald, Ann. "The Female Faust." In *Feminist Criticism: Essays on Theory, Poetry, and Prose,* edited by Cheryl L. Brown and Karen Olson, 211–21. Metuchen, N.J.: Scarecrow Press, 1978.

Rosaldo, Michelle Zimbalist. "Woman, Culture, and Society: A Theoretical Overview." In *Woman, Culture, and Society,* edited by Michelle Zimbalist Rosaldo and Louise Lamphere, 43–66. Palo Alto: Stanford University Press, 1974.

Rose, Ellen Cronan. "Through the Looking Glass: When Women Tell Fairy Tales." In *The Voyage In: Fictions of Female Development,* edited by Elizabeth Abel, Marianne Hirsch, and Elizabeth Langland, 209–27. Hanover & London: University Press of New England, 1983.

Rosinsky, Natalie M. "Mothers and Daughters: Another Minority Group." In *The Lost Tradition: Mothers and Daughters in Fiction,* edited by Cathy N. Davidson and E. M. Broner, 281–89. New York: Frederick Ungar, 1980.

———. *Feminist Futures: Contemporary Women's Speculative Fiction.* Ann Arbor, Mich.: UMI Research Press, 1984.

Rosowski, Susan J. "The Novel of Awakening." *Genre* 12, no.3 (Fall 1979): 313–32.

Rowe, Karen E. "Feminism and Fairy Tales." *Women's Studies* 6 (1979): 237–57.

Rubenstein, Roberta. *Boundaries of the Self: Gender, Culture, Fiction.* Urbana & Chicago: University of Illinois Press, 1987.

Ruddick, Sara. "Maternal Thinking." *Feminist Studies* 6, no.2 (Summer 1980): 342–67.

Russ, Joanna. "What Can a Heroine Do? Or Why Women Can't Write." In *Images of Women in Fiction: Feminist Perspectives,* edited by Susan Koppelman Cornillon. Bowling Green: Bowling Green University Popular Press, 1972.

Sammons, Jeffrey L. "The Mystery of the Missing *Bildungsroman,* or: What Happened to Wilhelm Meister's Legacy?" *Genre* XIV (Summer 1981): 229–46.

Samuels, Wilfrid D. "Liminality and the Search for Self in Toni Morrison's *Song of Solomon.*" *Minority Voices* 5, no.1/2 (Spring/ Fall 1981): 59–68.

Sander, Volkmar. "Der deutsche Bildungsroman in Amerika." *Deutsche-Rundschau* 87, no.11 (1961): 1,032–34.

Schafer, Roy. "Narration in the Psychoanalytic Dialogue." *Critical*

Inquiry 7, no.1 (Autumn 1980): 29–53.

Scholl, Margaret. *The Bildungsdrama of the Age of Goethe.* Frankfurt: Peter Lang, 1976.

Shaffner, Randolph P. *The Apprenticeship Novel.* Germanic Studies in America, no. 48. New York: Peter Lang, 1984.

Showalter, Elaine. "Literary Criticism." *Signs* 1, no.2 (1975): 435–60.

———. *A Literature of Their Own: British Women Novelists From Brontë to Lessing.* Princeton: Princeton University Press, 1977.

———. "Feminist Criticism in the Wilderness." *Critical Inquiry* 8, no.2 (Winter 1981): 179–205.

———., ed. *The New Feminist Criticism: Essays on Women, Literature Theory.* New York: Pantheon, 1985.

Smith, Barbara. "Toward a Black Feminist Criticism." In *Feminist Criticism and Social Change,* edited by G. Newton and D. Rosenfelt, 3–20. New York: Methuen, 1985.

Smith, Henry Nash. "The Scribbling Women and the Cosmic Success Story." *Critical Inquiry* 1 (1974): 47–70.

Snitow, Ann Barr. "The Front Line: Notes on Sex in Novels by Women, 1969–1979." *Signs* 5, no.4 (1980): 702–18.

Sollors, Werner. *Beyond Ethnicity: Consent and Descent in American Culture.* New York: Oxford University Press, 1986.

Sowell, Thomas. "The Mexicans." *Ethnic America.* New York: Basic Books, 1981.

Spacks, Patricia Meyer. *The Female Imagination.* New York: Alfred A. Knopf, 1975.

———. "Introduction." In *Contemporary Women Novelists,* edited by Patricia Meyer Spacks, 1–17. Englewood Cliffs, N.J.: Prentice Hall, 1977.

———. *Myths of Youth and the Adult Imagination.* New York: Basic Books, 1981.

Spector Person, Ethel. "Sexuality as the Mainstay of Identity: Psychoanalytical Perspectives." *Signs* 5, no.4 (1980): 605–30.

Stevens, Wallace. *The Necessary Angel, Essays on Reality and Imagination.* New York: Vintage Books, 1951.

Stewart, Grace. *A New Mythos. The Novel of the Artist as Heroine 1877–1977.* St. Albans, Vt.: Eden Press Women's Publications, 1979.

Stimpson, Catharine R. "Ad/d Feminam: Women, Literature, and Society." In *Literature and Society,* edited by Edward W. Said, 174–92. Baltimore & London: Johns Hopkins University Press, 1980.

Stone, Kay F. "The Misuses of Enchantment: Controversies on the Significance of Fairy Tales." In *Women's Folklore, Women's Cul-*

ture, edited by Rosann A. Jordan and Susan J. Kalcik, 125–45. Philadelphia: University of Pennsylvania Press, 1985.

Swales, Martin. *The German Bildungsroman from Wieland to Hesse.* Princeton: Princeton University Press, 1978.

———. "The German *Bildungsroman* and the Great Tradition." In *Comparative Criticism,* edited by Elinor Shaffer, 91–105. Cambridge: Cambridge University Press, 1979.

Tennyson, G. B. "The Bildungsroman in Nineteenth-Century English Literature." In *Medieval Epic to the "Epic Theater" of Brecht,* edited by Rosario P. Armato and John M. Spalek, 135–46. Los Angeles: University of Southern California Press, 1968.

Voloshin, Beverly R. "The Limits of Domesticity: The Female *Bildungsroman* in America, 1820–1870." *Women's Studies* 10, no.3 (1984): 283–302.

von Franz, Marie-Louise. *Individuation in Fairytales.* Dallas, Tex.: Spring Publications, 1977.

Wagner, Hans. *Der Englishe Bildungsroman Bis in die Zeit des Ersten Weltkrieges.* Diss. Zürich: Juris, 1951.

Wagner, Linda W. "Plath's *The Bell Jar* as Female *Bildungsroman.*" *Women's Studies* 12, no.1 (1986): 55–68.

Watt, Ian. *The Rise of the Novel.* Berkeley & Los Angeles: University of California Press, 1957.

Waxman, Barbara Frey. "From *Bildungsroman* to *Reifungsroman*: Aging in Doris Lessing's Fiction." *Soundings* LXVIII, no. 3 (Fall 1985): 318–34.

Wellek, René, and Austin Warren. *Theory of Literature.* New York: Harcourt, Brace, 1956.

Wenzel, Hélène Vivienne. "Introduction to Luce Irigaray's 'And the One Doesn't Stir Without the Other.'" *Signs* 7, no.1 (1981): 56–67.

White, Barbara A. *Growing Up Female: Adolescent Girlhood in American Fiction.* Westport, Conn.: Greenwood Press, 1985.

White, Hayden. "The Value of Narrativity in the Representation of Reality." *Critical Inquiry* 7, no.1 (Autumn 1980): 5–27.

Williamson, Marilyn I. "Toward a Feminist Literary History." *Signs* 10, no.1 (1984): 136–47.

Woolf, Virginia. *A Room of One's Own.* New York: Harcourt Brace Jovanovich, 1929.

———. "Professions for Women," *The Death of the Moth and Other Essays,* 226-38. New York: Harcourt Brace, 1942.

Wordsworth, William. "Prefaces." *The Poetical Works of William Wordsworth.* Edited by Thomas Hutchinson, 934–58. London: Oxford University Press, 1910.

Zipes, Jack. *The Trials and Tribulations of Little Red Riding Hood.*

South Hadley, Mass.: Berger and Garvey, 1983.

Chicana

Alarcón, Norma. "Chicana's Feminist Literature: A Re-Vision through Malintzin/or Malintzin: Putting Flesh Back on the Object." In *This Bridge Called My Back: Writings by Radical Women of Color,* edited by Cherríe Moraga and Gloria Alzaldúa, 182–90. New York: Kitchen Table: Women of Color Press, 1981.

———. "Hay Que Inventarnos/We Must Invent Ourselves." *Third Women* 1 (1981): 4–6.

———. "What Kind of Lover Have You Made Me, Mother?: Towards a Theory of Chicanas' Feminism and Cultural Identity Through Poetry." In *Women of Color: Perspectives on Feminism and Identity,* edited by Audrey T. McCluskey, 85–109. Occasional Papers Series, no. 1.1. Bloomington, Ind.: Women's Studies Program, Indiana University Press, 1985.

———. "Chicana Writers and Critics in a Social Context: Towards a Contemporary Bibliography." *Third Woman* 4 (1989): 169–78.

———. "The Sardonic Powers of the Erotic in the Work of Ana Castillo." In *Breaking Boundaries: Latina Writing and Critical Readings,* edited by Asunción Horno-Delgado, Eliana Ortega, Nina M. Scott, and Nancy Saporta Sternbach, 94–107. Amherst: University of Massachusetts Press, 1989.

———. "The Theoretical Subject(s) of *This Bridge Called My Back* and Anglo-American Feminism." In *Making Face, Making Soul Haciendo Caras,* edited by Gloria Anzaldúa, 356–66. San Francisco: Aunt Lute Foundation Books, 1990.

Anzaldúa, Gloria. "Speaking in Tongues: A Letter to 3rd World Women Writers." In *This Bridge Called My Back: Writings by Radical Women of Color,* edited by Cherríe Moraga and Gloria Anzaldúa, 165–74. New York: Kitchen Table: Women of Color Press, 1981.

———. *Borderlands/La Frontera: The New Mestiza.* San Francisco, Calif.: Spinster/Aunt Lute, 1987.

Apodaca, Maria Linda. "A Double Edge Sword: Hispanas and Liberal Feminism." *Critica* 1, no.3 (Fall 1986): 96–114.

Armas, José. "A Classical Bibliographical Novel by Isabella Ríos." *De Colores* 4 (1980): 1–2.

Binder, Wolfgang, ed. *Partial Autobiographies: Interviews with Twenty Chicano Poets.* Erlangen, West Germany: Verlag Palm and Enke Erlangen, 1985.

Bruce-Novoa, Juan. "Portraits of the Chicana Artist as a Young Man.

The Making of the Author in Three Chicano Novels." In *Festival Flor y Canto II,* edited by Arnold C. Vento, Alurista, José Flores Peregrino et al., 150–61. Albuquerque, N.M.: Pajarito, 1979.

———. "Canonical and Noncanonical Texts." *The Americas Review* 14, no.3/4 (Fall/Winter 1986): 119–35.

———. "Eva Antonia Wilbur-Cruce: la autobiographia como '*Bildungsroman.*'" In *Mujer y Literatura Mexicana y Chicana: Culturas en contacto,* edited by Aralia López González, Amelia Malagamba, and Elena Urrutia, 219–32. Tijuana, Mexico: El Colegio de México, El Colegio de la Frontera Norte, 1990.

Campos Carr, Irene. "A Survey of Selected Literature on La Chicana." *NWSA Journal* 1, no.2 (Winter 1988/89): 253–73.

Candalaria, Cordelia. "La Malinche, Feminist Prototype." *Frontiers* 5, no.2 (1980): 1–6.

———. *Chicano Poetry, A Critical Introduction.* Westport, Conn.: Greenwood Press, 1986.

Caribí, Angels. "Developing a Sense of Place: Sandra Cisneros in *The House on Mango Street.*" *Anuari* d'Anglés X (1987): 111–17.

Castillo, Ana. "The Distortion of Desire." *Third Woman* 4 (1989): 147–50.

———. "The Evolution of Chicana Erotica." *Heresies* 24 (1990): 50–53.

Chávez, Denise. "Heat and Rain (Testimonio)." In *Breaking Boundaries: Latina Writing and Critical Readings,* edited by Asunción Horno-Delgado, Eliana Ortega, Nina M. Scott, and Nancy Saporta Sternbach, 27–32. Amherst: University of Massachusetts Press, 1989.

Cisneros, Sandra. "My Wicked Wicked Ways: The Chicana Writer's Struggle With Good and Evil. Or Las Hijas De La Malavida." Unpublished manuscript.

———. Cisneros, Sandra. "Sandra Cisneros." In *Partial Autobiographies: Interviews with Twenty Chicano Poets,* edited and with an Introduction, a Glossary, & Bibliographies by Wolfgang Binder, 54–74. Erlangen, Germany. Verlag Palm & Enke, 1985.

———. "Notes to a Young(er) Writer." *The American Review* 15, no.1 (Spring 1987): 74–76.

Córdova, Teresa, et al., eds. *Chicana Voices: Intersections of Class, Race, and Gender.* Colorado Springs: The National Association for Chicano Studies, 1990.

Curiel, Barbara Brinson. "Lucha Corpi." *Chicano Writers.* First Series. Vol. 82, *Dictionary of Literary Bibliography,* edited by Francisco A Lomelí and Carl R. Shirley, 91–97. Detroit, Mich.: Gale Research, 1989.

De Alva, Jorge Klor. "Critique of National Character Vs. Universality in Chicana Poetry." *De Colores* 3, no.3 (1977): 20–24.

Enríquez, Evangelina. "Towards a Definition of, and Critical Approaches to Chicano(a) Literature." Ph.D. diss., University of California, Riverside, 1982.

Eysturoy, Annie O. "Isabella Ríos." *Chicano Writers*. First Series. Vol. 82, *Dictionary of Literary Bibliography*, edited by Francisco A. Lomelí and Carl R. Shirley, 201–05. Detroit, Mich: Gale Research, 1989.

——. "Denise Chávez." In *This Is About Vision: Interviews With Southwestern Writers*, edited by John F. Crawford, William Balassi, and Annie O. Eysturoy, 157–69. Albuquerque: University of New Mexico Press, 1990.

—— and José Antonio Gurpegui. "Chicano Literature: Introduction and Bibliography." *American Studies International* 28, no.1 (1990): 48–83.

Fisher, Jerilyn. "From Under the Yoke of Race and Sex: Black and Chicano Women's Fiction of the Seventies." *Minority Voices* 2, no.2 (Fall 1978): 1–13.

Gaitan, Marcella Trujillo. "The Dilemma of the Modern Chicana Artist and Critic." *De Colores* 3, no.3 (1977): 38–48.

Gonzalez, LaVerne. "Estela Portillo Trambley (1936–)." In *Chicano Literature: A Reference Guide*, edited by J. A. Martinez and F. A. Lomalí, 316–22. Westport, Conn: Greenwood Press, 1985.

Gonzales, Sylvia Alicia. "National Character vs. Universality in Chicano Poetry." *De Colores* 1, no.4 (1975): 10–21.

——. "Congress of Interamerican Women Writers—An Overview." *De Colores* 3, no.3 (1977): 8–19.

——. "Toward a Feminist Pedagogy for Chicana Self-Actualization." *Frontiers* 5, no.2 (1980): 48–51.

Gonzales-Berry, Erlinda. "Unveiling Athena: Women in the Chicano Novel." Unpublished manuscript.

——, and Tey Diana Rebolledo. "Growing Up Chicano: Tomás Rivera and Sandra Cisneros." *Revista Chicano-Riqueña* 13, no.3/4 (1985): 109–19.

Gutiérrez, Jess. "A Novel That Grew in the Streets of Oxnard." *Star Free Press*, 9 January 1977.

Gutierrez-Revuelto, Pedro. "Género e ideología en el libro de Sandra Cisneros: *The House on Mango Street*." *Critica* 1, no.3 (Fall 1986): 48–59.

Herrera-Sobek, María. *Beyond Stereotypes: The Critical Analysis of Chicana Literature*. Binghamton, N.Y.: Bilingual Press/Editorial Bilingüe, 1985.

———. "The Politics of Rape: Sexual Transgression in Chicana Fiction." In *Chicana Creativity: Charting New Frontiers in American Literature*, edited by María Herrera-Sobek and Helena María Viramontes, 171–81. Houston, Tex.: Arte Público Press, 1988.

———, and Helena María Viramontes, eds. *Chicana Creativity: Charting New Frontiers in American Literature*. Houston, Tex.: Arte Público Press, 1988.

Horno-Delgado, Asunción, Eliana Ortega, Nina M. Scott, and Nancy Saporta Sternbach, eds. *Breaking Boundaries: Latina Writing and Critical Readings*. Amherst: University of Massachusetts Press, 1989.

Jiménez, Francisco, ed. *The Identification and Analysis of Chicano Literature*. New York: Bilingual Press / Editorial Bilingüe, 1979.

Job, Peggy. "La sexualidad en la narrativa feminina mexicana 1970–1987: Una aproximación." *Third Woman* 4 (1989): 120–33.

Lattin, Patricia and Vernon. "Power and Freedom in the Stories of Estela Portillo Trambley." *Critique* 21, no.1 (Fall 1979): 93–101.

Leal, Luis. "Mexican American Literature: A Historical Perspective." In *Modern Chicano Writers: A Collection of Critical Essays*, edited by J. Sommers and T. Ybarra-Fausto, 18-30. Englewood Cliffs, N.J.: Prentice Hall, 1979.

——— and Pepe Barrón. "Chicano Literature: An Overview." In *Three American Literatures*, edited by Houston Baker, 9–32. New York: Modern Language Association of America, 1982.

Limón, José. "*La Llorona*, the Third Legend of Greater Mexico: Cultural Symbols, Women, and the Political Unconscious." *Renato Rosaldo Lecture Series*, Monograph 2, 53–94. Tucson: Mexican American Research Center, University of Arizona, 1986.

Lomelí, Francisco A. "Isabella Ríos and the Chicano Psychic Novel." *Minority Voices: An Interdisciplinary Journal of Literature and the Arts* 4 (Spring 1980): 49–61.

———. "Chicana Novelists in the Process of Creating Fictive Voices." In *Beyond Stereotypes*, edited by María Herrera-Sobek, 29–46. Binghamton, N.Y.: Bilingual Press/Editorial Bilingüe, 1985.

Lorenzana, Noemi. "La Chicana: Transcending the Old and Carving Out a New Life and Self-Image." *De Colores* 2, no.3 (1975): 6–14.

Luna Lawhn, Juanita. "*El Regidor* and *La Prensa*: Impediments to Women's Self-Definition." *Third Woman* 4 (1989): 134–42.

Lyon, Ted. "'Loss of Innocence' in Chicano Prose." In *The Identification and Analysis of Chicano Literature*, edited by Francisco Jiménez, 254–62. New York: Bililngual Press/Editorial Bilingüe, 1979.

McCluskey, Audrey T., ed. *Women of Color: Perspectives on Feminism and Identity.* Occasional Papers Series, no. 1.1. Bloomington, Ind.: Women's Studies Program, Indiana University, 1985.

McCracken, Ellen. "Sandra Cisneros' *The House on Mango Street:* Community-Oriented Introspection and the Demystification of Patriarchal Violence." In *Breaking Boundaries: Latina Writing and Critical Readings,* edited by Asunción Horno-Delgado, Eliana Oretega, Nina M. Scott, and Nancy Saporta Sternbach, 62–71. Amherst: University of Massachusetts Press, 1989.

Martínez, Julio A., and Francisco A. Lomelí, eds. *Chicano Literature: A Reference Guide.* Westport, Conn.: Greenwood Press, 1985.

Martín-Rodríguez, Manuel M. "The Book of 'Mango Street': escritura y liberación en la obra de Sandra Cisneros." In *Mujer y Literatura Mexicana y Chicana: Culturas en contacto,* edited by Aralia López González, Amelia Malagamba, y Elena Urrutia, 249–54. Tijuana, Mexico: El Colegio de México, El Colegio de la Frontera Norte, 1990.

Moraga, Cherríe. "Algo secretamente amado." *Third Woman* 4 (1989): 151–56.

———. "The Obedient Daughter." *Third Woman* 4 (1989): 157–62.

———, and Gloria Anzaldúa, eds. *This Bridge Called My Back: Writings by Radical Women of Color.* New York: Kitchen Table: Women of Color Press, 1981.

Olivares, Julián. "Sandra Cisneros' *The House on Mango Street,* and the Poetics of Space." In *Chicana Creativity: Charting New Frontiers in American Literature,* edited by María Herrera-Sobek and Helena María Viramontes, 160–70. Houston, Tex.: Arte Público Press, 1988.

Ordóñez, Elizabeth. "Narrative Texts by Ethnic Women: Rereading the Past, Reshaping the Future." *MELUS* 7, no. 4 (Winter 1980): 19–28.

———. "Sexual Politics and the Theme of Sexuality in Chicana Poetry." In *Women in Hispanic Literature: Icons and Fallen Idols,* edited by Beth Miller, 316–39. Berkeley: University of California Press, 1983.

———. "Alma Villanueva (1944–)." In *Chicano Literature: A Reference Guide,* edited by J. A. Martinez and F. A. Lomelí, 413–20. Westport, Conn.: Greenwood Press, 1985.

Ortega, Eliana, and Nancy Saporta Sternbach. "At the Threshold of the Unnamed: Latina Literary Discourse in the Eighties." In *Breaking Boundaries: Latina Writing and Critical Readings,* edited by Asunción Horno-Delgado, Eliana Ortega, Nina M. Scott, and Nancy Saporta Sternbach, 2–19. Amherst: University of Massachusetts Press, 1989.

Paredes, Raymond A. "The Evolution of Chicano Literature." In *Three American Literatures,* edited by Houston A. Baker, 33–79. New York: Modern Language Association of America, 1982.

Parr, Carmen Salazar, and Genevieve M. Ramirez. "Surrealism in the Work of Estela Portillo." *MELUS* 7, no.4 (Winter 1980): 85–92.

———. "The Chicana in Chicano Literature." In *Chicano Literature: A Reference Guide,* edited by Julio A. Martinez and Francisco A. Lomelí, 97–107. Westport, Conn.: Greenwood Press, 1985.

———. "The Female Hero in Chicano Literature." In *Beyond Stereotypes: The Critical Analysis of Chicana Literature,* edited by María Herrera-Sobek, 47–60. Binghamton, N.Y.: Bilingual Press/ Editorial Bilingüe, 1985.

Paz, Octavio. *The Labyrinth of Solitude.* New York: Grove Press, 1985.

Portillo, Estela. "Introduction." *El Grito* 7, no.1 (1973): 3–6.

Quintana, Alvina. "Expanding a Feminist View: Challenge and Counter-Challenge in the Relationship Between Women." *Revista Mujeres* 2, no.1 (Jan. 1985): 11–18.

———. "La lucha continúa." *Third Woman* 4 (1989): 163–65.

Rebolledo, Tey Diana. "The Bittersweet Nostalgia of Childhood in the Poetry of Margarita Cota-Cárdenas." *Frontiers* 5, no.2 (1980): 31–35.

———. "Soothing Restless Serpents: The Dreaded Creation and Other Inspirations in Chicana Poetry." *Third Woman* 2, no.1 (1984): 83–102.

———. "Tradition and Mythology: Signatures of Landscape in Chicana Literature." In *The Desert Is No Lady: Southwestern Landscapes in Women's Writing and Art,* edited by Vera Norwood and Janice Monk, 96–124. New Haven: Yale University Press, 1987.

———. "Abuelitas: Mythology and Integration in Chicana Literature." In *Woman of Her Word: Hispanic Women Write,* edited by Evangelina Vigil, 148–58. Houston, Tex.: Arte Público Press, 1987.

———. "Hispanic Women Writers of the Southwest: Tradition and Innovation." In *Old Southwest/New Southwest: Essays on a Region and Its Literature,* edited by Judy N. Lensink, 49–61. Tucson, Ariz.: Bilingual Press, 1987.

Riccatelli, R. "The Sexual Stereotypes of the Chicana in Literature." *Encuentro Femenil* 1, no.2 (1974): 48–56.

Ridell, Adaljiza Sosa. "Chicanas and El Movimiento." *Aztlan* 5, no.1/2 (Spring/Fall 1974): 155–65.

Rincon, Bernice. "La Chicana: Her Role in the Past and Her Search for a New Role in the Future." *Regeneración* 1, no.10 (1971):

15–18.

Rivera, Tomás. "Chicano Literature: Fiesta of the Living." In *The Identification and Analysis of Chicano Literature*, edited by Francisco Jiménez, 19–36. New York: Bilingual Press/Editorial Bilingüe, 1979.

———. "Chicano Literature: The Establishment of Community." In *A Decade of Chicano Literature (1970–1979): Critical Essays and Bibliography*, edited by Luis Leal et al., 9–17. Santa Barbara, Calif.: Editorial La Causa, 1982.

Roccard, Marcienne. "The Chicana: A Marginal Woman." In *European Perspectives on Hispanic Literature of the United States*, edited by Genvieve Fabre, 150–59. Houston, Tex.: Arte Público Press, 1988.

———. "The Remembering Voice in Chicana Literature." In *European Perspectives on Hispanic Literature of the United States*, edited by Genvieve Fabre, 150–59. Houston, Tex.: Arte Público Press, 1988.

Rodriguez, Richard. "The New American Scholarship Boy." In *Introduction to Chicano Studies*, edited by Livie Isauro Duran and H. Russell Bernard, 364–74. New York: Macmillan, 1982.

Rosaldo, Renato. "Changing Chicano Narratives." In *Culture and Truth: The Remaking of Social Analysis*, 147-67. Boston: Beacon Press, 1989.

Saldívar, Ramón. "Ideologies of the Self: Chicano Autobiography." *Diacritics* 15, no.3 (Fall 1985): 25–34.

———. "The Dialectics of Subjectivity: Gender and Difference in Isabella Ríos, Sandra Cisneros, and Cherríe Moraga." In *Chicano Narrative: The Dialectics of Difference*, 171–99. Madison: University of Wisconsin Press, 1990.

Salinas, Judy. "The Role of Women in Chicano Literature." In *The Identification and Analysis of Chicano Literature*, edited by Francisco Jiménez, 191–240. New York: Bilingual Press/Editorial Bilingüe, 1979.

Sánchez, Maria Ester. *Contemporary Chicana Poetry: A Critical Approach to an Emerging Literature.* Berkeley, Calif.: University of California Press, 1985.

Sanchez, Rita. "Chicana Writer Breaking Out of Silence." *De Colores* 3, no.3 (1977): 31–37.

Seator, Lynette. "*Emplumada*: Chicana Rites-of-Passage." *MELUS* 11, no.2 (Summer 1984): 23–38.

Shirley, Carl R. "*Pocho*: Bildungsroman of a Chicano." *Revista Chicano-Riqueña* 7, no.2 (Spring 1979): 63–68.

Tafolla, Carmen. "Chicano Literature, Beyond Beginnings." In *South-*

ern Exposure 9, no.2 (1981): 206–25.

———. *To Split a Human: Mitos, Machos y la Mujer Chicana*. San Antonio, Tex.: Mexican American Cultural Center, 1985.

Treviño, Gloria Velásquez. "Cultural Ambivalence in Early Chicana Literature." In *European Perspectives on Hispanic Literature of the United States*, edited by Genvieve Fabre, 140–46. Houston, Tex.: Arte Público Press, 1988.

Vallejos, Thomas. "Ritual Process and the Family in the Chicano Novel." *MELUS* 10, no.4 (Winter 1983): 5–16.

———. "Estela Portillo Trambley's Fictive Search for Paradise." In *Contemporary Chicano Fiction: A Critical Survey*, edited by Vernon Lattin, 269–77. Binghamton, N.Y.: Bilingual Press/ Editorial Bilingüe, 1986.

Vigil, Evangelina, ed. *Woman of Her Word: Hispanic Women Write*. Houston, Tex.: Arte Público Press, 1987.

Viramontes, Helena Maria. "'Nopalitos': The Making of Fiction (Testimonio)." In *Breaking Boundaries: Latina Writing and Critical Readings*, edited by Asunción Horno-Delgado, Eliana Ortega, Nina M. Scott, and Nancy Saporta Sternbach, 33–38. Amherst: University of Massachusetts Press, 1989.

von Bardeleben, Renate, Dietrich Briesemeister, and Juan Bruce-Novoa, eds. *Missions in Conflict: Essays on U.S.-Mexican Relations and Chicano Culture*. Tübingen: Gunter Narr Verlag, 1986.

Yarbro-Bejarano, Yvonne. "Chicana Literature from a Chicana Feminist Perspective." In *Chicana Creativity: Charting New Frontiers in American Literature*, edited by María Herrera-Sobek and Helena María Viramontes, 139–45. Houston, Tex.: Arte Público Press, 1988.

Zamora, Bernice. "The Chicana as a Literary Critic." *De Colores* 3, no.3 (1977): 16–19.

Zavella, Patricia. "The Problematic Relationship of Feminism and Chicana Studies. *Women's Studies* 17 (1989): 25–36.

Zinn, Maxine Baca. "Chicanas: Power and Control in the Domestic Sphere." *De Colores* 2, no.3 (Spring 1975): 19–31.

———. "Gender and Ethnic Identity among Chicanos." *Frontiers* 5, no.2 (1980): 18–24.

INDEX

Accommodation, male, 29
Adolescents, church and, 63–64;
  novels about, 17–18
Aging, 119
Ahijados, 124
Alienation: entrapment and, 136;
  from gender-role norms, 19;
  house as symbol of, 92–93; of
  immigrant, 77; in *Menu Girls*,
  126–27; of self, 81; theme of
  male, 10; in United States, 78; in
  Victuum, 53
American Book Award, 89
Anaya, Rodolfo, 11, 134
Anglos: at border, 125; oppressive
  world of, 123; pimps, 48;
  prejudice in *Mango*, 92, 100;
  prejudice in *Victuum*, 46;
  scholarship of feminist, 25;
  stereotypes by, 133; violation of
  nature by, 115
Aristotle, 7
Artists, 21–23, 90
Authoritarianism, 43–46
Authority, female narrative, 86
Authorship, anxiety of, 55
Autobiography, 4

Bachelard, Gaston, 104, 110–11
Barrio, 89–92; in *Menu Girls*, 113;
  negative analogy with, 94; return
  to, 108–9, 111, 130
Becoming, theme of, 3, 138
Bildung: Chicana, 85, 128;
  communal significance and,

112; concept of, 7–8; and
  entrapment, 81; historical
  concept of, 7–8, 9; in *Mango*,
  107; mother-daughter relationship and, 116–17; patriarchy
  and, 135; psychic, 53; socio-
  cultural environment and, 123;
  translation of, 59; in *Trini*, 58; in
  Victuum, 54; writing and, 129–30
Bildungsheld: Anglo definitions
  and, 26; Chicana, 137; Chicano
  definitions and, 26; construction
  of self and, 111; male, 8; sexual
  "other" of, 15; in *Trini*, 78
Bildungsroman: andocentric
  approaches to, 13; Chicana, 5,
  87, 137; city nd, 71–72; community of women and, 11; concept
  of, 5–7; conclusion of, 20–21;
  ethnic identity and, 134–35; as
  female genre, 5; female heroines
  and, 18; first by Chicana, 33;
  gender and, 133; genre, 3;
  historical examples of, 7; intent
  of traditional, 29; as journey, 4;
  nature and, 114–15; oppression
  and, 133–34; patriarchal
  definitions and, 85–86; sexual
  initiation, 66; thematic features
  of, 11; tradition transformed, 27;
  women's, 5
Biography, 36
Border, 75–76, 113, 125–26
Breathing, process of, 92

Cabeza de Vaca, Fabiola, 34–35
California, 36–37, 46, 83
Campbell, Joseph, 52, 58, 64–65, 68, 76
Casitas, 69, 71
Catholic church, 63–64, 78
Chicanas: developmental process of, 27; fictional themes of, 3; negative image of, 59; political generations of, 35–56; stereotypes of, 24–25, 109
Chicano Movement, 33
Chingada, 67
Chopin, Kate, 7, 83
Christianity, 23, 63
Citizenship, 75
City as source of corruption, 71–72
Cixous, Hélène, 39
Closets as symbols, 115–16
Comadres, 42–43, 108, 113, 118, 124
Coming of age: becoming and, 3; in *Mango*, 89; in *Victuum*, 49
Communal relationships, 124–25
Community of women, 118; conspiracy of silence and, 100. *See also* Women
Compadres, 113, 124
Conservatism, social, 9
Corpi, Lucha, 7
Creativity, 21–22, 90, 106–7
Critical theory: feminist, 13–14, 25, 137; male, 13; radical, 14
Cultural expectations: in *Trini*, 30; in *Victuum*, 30
Curanderas, 41

Daughters, obedient, 30. *See also* Mother-daughter relationships
Depression, the Great, 37
Dialogue, novels of, 37
Dilthey, Wilhelm, 8
Dinesen, Isak, 25
Disease, female, 119–20
Domestication, 43
Domesticity, passive, 30

Dominant culture, stereotypes of Chicanas in, 24–25
Drama, rhetoric of, 37–38
Dreams, 52
Duendes, 60
Dwarf character, 75–76

Economic dependency of poor women: as catalyst, 130; in *Mango*, 101–2; and psychological, 82, 116, 135–36; in *Trini*, 69, 74
Economy, foreign interests in Mexico's, 63, 64
Education, college, 126
El Espejo, 59
Entrapment: alienation and, 136; image of, 101; in *Mango*, 89; resistance to, 30–31, 88, 128–29; return to nature and, 82; in *Victuum*, 50; women's position and, 81
Esperanza, significance of name of, 95–96, 108–9
Eternal Feminine, 14–15
Ethnic consciousness, 55, 110, 125, 135, 137; creation and, 131
Ethnic pride, 48

Family: collective identity of, 90–91; solidarity, 48; traditional, 105
Female bonding, 70
Female conditioning, traditional, 64
Female development: green world archetype of, 62; myth of heroine and, 58; nature of, 129; race and class in, 134; rape-trauma archetype, 67–68; sociocultural realities and, 83; submerged meanings and, 36
Female sexuality, 98–101
Feminine ideal, 14, 121
Femininity text, 30
Feminism: exclusivism of, 25–26;

Madness, danger of, 53
Madres abnegadas, 105
Madrinas, 124
Male authority, 41–42, 43–46
Male autonomy, assumption of, 29
Male force, beastly, 103–4, 120–21
Male prerogatives, 11–13, 66
Malinche, 67
Mann, Thomas, 8
Marina, Doña, 67
Marriage: happy endings and, 79–80; inevitability of, 80; maternity and, 30; patriarchy and, 42; in *Trini*, 74; in *Victuum*, 49–50
Marshall, Paule, 7
Meanings, submerged, 49, 50–51
Mestizas, 66; cultural conflicts of, 78; identity of, 68
Mexico, 57, 59–60, 125
Minority: dual identity, 48; silent, 37
Mistresses, 69, 71
Mojados, 110
Monomyths, 64–65, 76
Morgenstern, Karl, 6
Mothers, death of, 51, 60–61
Mother-daughter relationships, 40, 51, 52, 115–18, 127–28. *See also* Daughters, obedient; *Madres abnegadas*; Mothers, death of; Motherhood
Motherhood: psychic connection and, 41; symbolic, 40
Mujeriegos, 70
Mythic, undertones of, 57
Myths, patterns of, 22

Narrators, elimination of, 37
Nature: identification with, 77–78, 94–95, 114–15; love of, 61; return to, 82
Networks, female, 50. *See also* Women
New Mexico, 113, 130, 134
Nostalgia, Hispanic, 34

Novels: Chicano, 10; didactic, 6; first Chicana, 33; of pure dialogue, 37. *See also* Literature

Opposition, strategy of, 36
Oral traditions, 33–34, 37–38; in *Victuum*, 38
Otherness, 19
Outsiders, societal, 10

Patriarchal poetics, 30, 36, 110
Patriarchy: acceptance of, 77; alienation from, 77; complicity of women in, 42; doctrines of female behavior and, 41–42; female *Bildung* and, 18–20; female sexuality and, 44; independence and, 79; internalization and, 102, 121; oppression and, 135; resistance to, 97; social conditioning and, 54; socio-cultural ideology of, 29
Patrona, 124
Paz, Octavio, 67
Pen names, use of, 55
Phallocentrism, 102
Pimps, 48
Poverty, 91–94, 107–8
Prohibition, 37
Prostitutes, 46, 47, 65, 75. *See also* Whores
Protagonists as narrators, 86–87
Psychic gifts, 41, 50–53, 81
Psycho-mythological interpretations, 52–53

Quest: for identity, 57; male, 31; mythic, 64; myths, 79; social, 53; spiritual, 53, 54
Quest, female: design of, 76; entrapment and, 109; ethnic contexts of, 134; heroic, 15, 58; narrative authority and, 128; subversion of traditional, 86; transformation of, 133

Rape: collective, 67; helplessness and, 65–66, 67; in *Mango*, 99–101; metaphor of, 66–67; rape-trauma archetype, 16, 67–68. *See also* Violation, sexual
Realism, social, 79–80
Rebellion, female, 16, 19
Rebirth, 88
Reincarnation, 52
Rites of passage: concept of, 3; in *Menu Girls*, 113; myth and, 64; psychic, 52–53; social and environmental influences on, 4
Rivalry, female, 70, 71
Rivera, Tomás, 11, 37–38, 48, 104–5, 134,
Role models, female, 116–17; lack of, 122; in *Mango*, 99–100, 101; in *Menu Girls*, 120–22; in *Trini*, 70
Role models, male, 43–44
Role of Hispanic community, 37–38
Romance, social realism and, 79–80

Salinger, J.D., 7
Self development, path toward, 4, 6
Self divided, 55
Self-assertion, creative, 23
Self-creation, 38, 40
Self-definition, 40
Self-development: creative imagination and, 88; facets of female, 20; and female *Bildungsroman*, 15–21; female paradigms of, 21; path toward, 4, 6; process of, 3; in *Victuum*, 38
Self-discovery, contradictions of, 87
Self-mutilation, 47
Self-reliance, 75
Self-representation, 26
Self-sacrifice, 76–77, 106
Sensuality, emergence of, 62–63, 98–101, 120

Sexual freedom, 15
Sexual initiation, 65–66, 100
Sexual violence: in *Mango*, 99–101; in *Victuum*, 47–48
Sexuality, control over, 44, 98–101, 103
Silence: act of, 39; breaking the, 24, 33; conspiracy of, 100–101
Smedley, Agnes, 7
Social roles, 16–17
Society as locus for experience, 6
Spain, identification with, 34
Spirituality, female, 50–53
Subjectivity, 88, 128, 131
Submission, ideology of, 42
Support systems, female, 40–41, 42

Taming of female adolescents, 43–44, 49, 105–6
Tarahumara Indians, 61
Texas, 58
Tonzantzín, 77–78

United States: Chicano experience in, 134; migration to, 57–58, 60, 75, 83

Venus, myth of, 67
Victimization: gradual, 49; men and, 72; sacrificial, 17; self affirmation and, 136; social, 50; in *Victuum*, 53–54
Victuum: literary strategies of, 36–37; meaning of title of, 53–54; as transitional, 35–36
Villarreal, José Antonio, 7, 11
Violation, sexual, 65, 66, 68. *See also* Rape
Violence, domestic, 48, 103
Virginity, 44, 63

Warren, Nina Otero, 34
Wetbacks, 125
Whores, 69–70. *See also* Prostitutes
Wolfe, Thomas, 7

Womanhood: cult of true, 14; male-imposed definitions of, 70; nature of, 120; as necessary "other", 12–13, 14; norms of, 30; as objects for creation, 22; patriarchal concepts of, 42, 43–44; as sinners or saints, 15; stereotypes of, 14, 15, 24–25; traditional roles of Hispanic, 34–35, 41; Women: family of, 118–19, 123. *See also Comadres*; Community of women; Networks, female; Support systems, female; Womanhood; Women writers

Women writers, 127–28, 136; objective of, 39; paradigms and, 87; protagonists as, 88

Woolf, Virginia, 117

World War II, 37

Zeitgeist, 6–7